19

J
92
Eisenh
ower   Sandberg, Peter Lar

Dwight D. Eisenhower

E

R

J
92
Eisenh
ower

DWIGHT D. EISENHOWER

Peter Lars Sandberg

1986
CHELSEA HOUSE PUBLISHERS
NEW YORK
NEW HAVEN   PHILADELPHIA

SENIOR EDITOR: William P. Hansen
ASSOCIATE EDITORS: Jane Crain
John Selfridge
Marian W. Taylor
EDITORIAL COORDINATOR: Karyn Gullen Browne
EDITORIAL STAFF: Pierre Hauser
Perry Scott King
Howard Ratner
Dan Sherer
Alma Rodriguez-Sokol
Bert Yaeger
ART DIRECTOR: Susan Lusk
LAYOUT: Irene Friedman
ART ASSISTANTS: Noreen Lamb
Victoria Tomaselli
COVER DESIGN: Frank Steiner
PICTURE RESEARCH: Carrie Bruns
Elizabeth Terhune

First Printing

Library of Congress Cataloging in Publication Data

Sandberg, Peter Lars. DWIGHT D. EISENHOWER

(World leaders past & present)
Bibliography: p.
Includes index
  1. Eisenhower, Dwight D. (Dwight David), 1890–1969—
Juvenile literature.   2. Presidents—United States—
Biography—Juvenile literature.   [1. Eisenhower,
Dwight D. (Dwight David), 1890–1969.   2. Presidents]
  I. Title.   II. Series.
E836.S26   1986   973.921′092′4 [B] [92]   86-2236

ISBN 0-87754-521-9

Chelsea House Publishers

Harold Steinberg, Chairman and Publisher
Susan Lusk, Vice President
A Division of Chelsea House Educational Communications, Inc.

133 Christopher Street, New York, NY 10014

345 Whitney Avenue, New Haven, CT 06510

5014 West Chester Pike, Edgemont, PA 19028

Photos courtesy of AP/ Wide World Photos, The Eisenhower Library, Library
of Congress, The National Archives, The Smithsonian Institution, UPI/Bett-
mann Newsphotos, U.S. Army, U.S. Navy

Contents

"On Leadership," Arthur M. Schlesinger, jr. 7

1. In Command 13
2. The Will to Win 19
3. Eisenhower's Luck. 29
4. The Warrior 41
5. Farm Boy to President 61
6. Crises Continue 89
7. An Old Soldier in a New Age 105

Further Reading 112
Chronology 113
Index 114

ON LEADERSHIP

Arthur M. Schlesinger, jr.

LEADERSHIP, it may be said, is really what makes the world go round. Love no doubt smooths the passage; but love is a private transaction between consenting adults. Leadership is a public transaction with history. The idea of leadership affirms the capacity of individuals to move, inspire and mobilize masses of people so that they act together in pursuit of an end. Sometimes leadership serves good purposes, sometimes bad; but whether the end is benign or evil, great leaders are those men and women who leave their personal stamp on history.

Now, the very concept of leadership implies the proposition that individuals can make a difference. This proposition has never been universally accepted. From classical times to the present day, eminent thinkers have regarded individuals as no more than the agents and pawns of larger forces, whether the gods and goddesses of the ancient world or, in the modern era, race, class, nation, the dialectic, the will of the people, the spirit of the times, history itself. Against such forces, the individual dwindles into insignificance.

So contends the thesis of historical determinism. Tolstoy's great novel *War and Peace* offers a famous statement of the case. Why, Tolstoy asked, did millions of men in the Napoleonic wars, denying their human feelings and their common sense, move back and forth across Europe slaughtering their fellows? "The war," Tolstoy answered, "was bound to happen simply because it was bound to happen." All prior history predetermined it. As for leaders, they, Tolstoy said, "are but the labels that serve to give a name to an end and, like labels, they have the least possible connection with the event." The greater the leader, "the more conspicuous the inevitability and the predestination of every act he commits." The leader, said Tolstoy, is "the slave of history."

Determinism takes many forms. Marxism is the determinism of class, Nazism the determinism of race. But the idea of men and women as the slaves of history runs athwart the deepest human instincts. Rigid determinism abolishes the idea of human freedom—the assumption of free choice that underlies every move we make, every word we speak, every thought we think. It abolishes the idea of human responsibility, since it is manifestly unfair to reward or punish people for actions that are by definition beyond their control. No one can live consistently by any deterministic creed. The Marxist states prove this themselves by their extreme susceptibility to the cult of leadership.

More than that, history refutes the idea that individuals make no difference. In December 1931 a British politician crossing Park Avenue in New York City between 76th and 77th Streets around ten-thirty at night looked in the wrong direction and was knocked down by an automobile—a moment, he later recalled, of a man aghast, a world aglare: "I do not understand why I was not broken like an eggshell or squashed like a gooseberry." Fourteen months later an American politician, sitting in an open car in Miami, Florida, was fired on by an assassin; the man beside him was hit. Those who believe that individuals make no difference to history might well ponder whether the next two decades would have been the same had Mario Contasini's car killed Winston Churchill in 1931 and Giuseppe Zangara's bullet killed Franklin Roosevelt in 1933. Suppose, in addition, that Adolf Hitler had been killed in the street fighting during the Munich *Putsch* of 1923 and that Lenin had died of typhus during the First World War. What would the 20th century be like now?

For better or for worse, individuals do make a difference. "The notion that a people can run itself and its affairs anonymously," wrote the philosopher William James, "is now well known to be the silliest of absurdities. Mankind does nothing save through initiatives on the part of inventors, great or small, and imitation by the rest of us—these are the sole factors in human progress. Individuals of genius show the way, and set the patterns, which common people then adopt and follow."

Leadership, James suggests, means leadership in thought as well as in action. In the long run, leaders in thought may well make the greater difference to the world. But, as Woodrow Wilson once said, "Those only are leaders of men, in the general eye, who lead in action. . . . It is at their hands that new thought gets its translation into the crude language of deeds." Leaders in thought often invent in solitude and obscurity, leaving to later generations the tasks of imitation. Leaders in action—the leaders portrayed in this series—have to be effective in their own time.

And they cannot be effective by themselves. They must act in response to the rhythms of their age. Their genius must be adapted, in a phrase of William James's, "to the receptivities of the moment." Leaders are useless without followers. "There goes the mob," said the French politician hearing a clamor in the streets. "I am their leader. I must follow them." Great leaders turn the inchoate emotions of the mob to purposes of their own. They seize on the opportunities of their time, the hopes, fears, frustrations, crises, potentialities.

8

They succeed when events have prepared the way for them, when the community is waiting to be aroused, when they can provide the clarifying and organizing ideas. Leadership ignites the circuit between the individual and the mass and thereby alters history.

It may alter history for better or for worse. Leaders have been responsible for the most extravagant follies and most monstrous crimes that have beset suffering humanity. They have also been vital in such gains as humanity has made in individual freedom, religious and racial tolerance, social justice and respect for human rights.

There is no sure way to tell in advance who is going to lead for good and who for evil. But a glance at the gallery of men and women in *World Leaders—Past and Present* suggests some useful tests.

One test is this: do leaders lead by force or by persuasion? By command or by consent? Through most of history leadership was exercised by the divine right of authority. The duty of followers was to defer and to obey. "Theirs not to reason why,/ Theirs but to do and die." On occasion, as with the so-called "enlightened despots" of the 18th century in Europe, absolutist leadership was animated by humane purposes. More often, absolutism nourished the passion for domination, land, gold and conquest and resulted in tyranny.

The great revolution of modern times has been the revolution of equality. The idea that all people should be equal in their legal condition has undermined the old structures of authority, hierarchy and deference. The revolution of equality has had two contrary effects on the nature of leadership. For equality, as Alexis de Tocqueville pointed out in his great study *Democracy in America*, might mean equality in servitude as well as equality in freedom.

"I know of only two methods of establishing equality in the political world," Tocqueville wrote. "Rights must be given to every citizen, or none at all to anyone . . . save one, who is the master of all." There was no middle ground "between the sovereignty of all and the absolute power of one man." In his astonishing prediction of 20th-century totalitarian dictatorship, Tocqueville explained how the revolution of equality could lead to the "*Führerprinzip*" and more terrible absolutism than the world had ever known.

But when rights are given to every citizen and the sovereignty of all is established, the problem of leadership takes a new form, becomes more exacting than ever before. It is easy to issue commands and enforce them by the rope and the stake, the concentration camp and the *gulag*. It is much harder to use argument and achievement to overcome opposition and win consent. The Founding Fathers of the United States understood the difficulty. They believed that history had given them the opportunity to decide, as

Alexander Hamilton wrote in the first Federalist Paper, whether men are indeed capable of basing government on "reflection and choice, or whether they are forever destined to depend . . . on accident and force."

Government by reflection and choice called for a new style of leadership and a new quality of followership. It required leaders to be responsive to popular concerns, and it required followers to be active and informed participants in the process. Democracy does not eliminate emotion from politics; sometimes it fosters demagoguery; but it is confident that, as the greatest of democratic leaders put it, you cannot fool all of the people all of the time. It measures leadership by results and retires those who overreach or falter or fail.

It is true that in the long run despots are measured by results too. But they can postpone the day of judgment, sometimes indefinitely, and in the meantime they can do infinite harm. It is also true that democracy is no guarantee of virtue and intelligence in government, for the voice of the people is not necessarily the voice of God. But democracy, by assuring the rights of opposition, offers built-in resistance to the evils inherent in absolutism. As the theologian Reinhold Niebuhr summed it up, "Man's capacity for justice makes democracy possible, but man's inclination to injustice makes democracy necessary."

A second test for leadership is the end for which power is sought. When leaders have as their goal the supremacy of a master race or the promotion of totalitarian revolution or the acquisition and exploitation of colonies or the protection of greed and privilege or the preservation of personal power, it is likely that their leadership will do little to advance the cause of humanity. When their goal is the abolition of slavery, the liberation of women, the enlargement of opportunity for the poor and powerless, the extension of equal rights to racial minorities, the defense of the freedoms of expression and opposition, it is likely that their leadership will increase the sum of human liberty and welfare.

Leaders have done great harm to the world. They have also conferred great benefits. You will find both sorts in this series. Even "good" leaders must be regarded with a certain wariness. Leaders are not demigods; they put on their trousers one leg after another just like ordinary mortals. No leader is infallible, and every leader needs to be reminded of this at regular intervals. Irreverence irritates leaders but is their salvation. Unquestioning submission corrupts leaders and demeans followers. Making a cult of a leader is always a mistake. Fortunately hero worship generates its own antidote. "Every hero," said Emerson, "becomes a bore at last."

The signal benefit the great leaders confer is to embolden the rest of us to live according to our own best selves, to be active, insistent, and resolute in affirming our own sense of things. For great leaders attest to the reality of human freedom against the supposed inevitabilities of history. And they attest to the wisdom and power that may lie within the most unlikely of us, which is why Abraham Lincoln remains the supreme example of great leadership. A great leader, said Emerson, exhibits new possibilities to all humanity. "We feed on genius. . . . Great men exist that there may be greater men."

Great leaders, in short, justify themselves by emancipating and empowering their followers. So humanity struggles to master its destiny, remembering with Alexis de Tocqueville: "It is true that around every man a fatal circle is traced beyond which he cannot pass; but within the wide verge of that circle he is powerful and free; as it is with man, so with communities."

—*New York*

1

In Command

You are about to embark upon the Great Crusade. The eyes of the world are upon you.
—DWIGHT D. EISENHOWER speaking to his troops, giving the order to launch the invasion of Normandy, June 5, 1944

June 5, 1944. The world is at war. The German armies have occupied France, Belgium, Luxembourg, the Netherlands, Norway, and Denmark. In southern England the Allied forces are poised, ready to strike what they hope will be the final blow against the German armies on the Western Front. The time is 3:30 A.M.

In his command trailer near Portsmouth, on the south coast of England, General Dwight D. Eisenhower has just awakened to the sounds of terrific wind and rain. Before going to sleep, he had prayed for a break in the weather. His prayers have not been answered.

Eisenhower gets up, dons his uniform, and prepares to drive to nearby Southwick House, where his top military advisers are already gathering. Usually outgoing and optimistic, known for his cheerfulness and broad grin, Eisenhower is in a somber mood today. As supreme commander of the Allied Expeditionary Force in Europe, he knows he will have to decide within the next hour whether or not to launch what would be the greatest air and sea invasion in the history of the world.

General Dwight Eisenhower (1890–1969) watches a tank gunnery test at an artillery range in England in 1944, shortly before the Allied invasion of German-occupied Europe. Eisenhower oversaw the invasion that put a stop to the German war machine and helped end World War II.

German dictator Adolf Hitler (1889–1945) whose Nazi party was swept into power in 1933 by rising German nationalism. His regime was based on political repression, militarism, and violent anti-Semitism.

American troops board a landing craft, making their way from southern England to the coast of France as part of the D-Day operation. The attack on German fortifications along the shores of Normandy was the most dramatic and decisive confrontation in modern history.

He believes the success of the invasion of France will depend on favorable tides in the English Channel and on fair weather. Today the tides are perfect. But as he steps out of his trailer and feels the full force of the wind and rain, he thinks the weather could not be worse. Because of it, he has already had to delay the invasion once. Now he knows he may have to delay it again, and this is the last thing in the world he wants to do.

Across the English Channel, all along the Normandy coast of France, German armies commanded by Field Marshal Erwin Rommel are waiting in their heavily fortified positions. Under Rommel's supervision, military engineers have been covering the beaches with anti-invasion obstacles since February. These obstacles include rows of wooden posts driven into the sand and topped with explosive charges, lengths of angle iron welded into "hedgehogs" and strewn along the tidal flats, barbed wire fences, mine fields, and huge wood and steel barricades facing the sea.

Rommel and the other German generals know the Allies are preparing to launch an invasion, but they do not know exactly where or when. With the passing of each day, their coastal defenses are getting stronger. These defenses are part of what Adolf Hitler, Germany's dictatorial ruler, calls his "Atlantic Wall." Hitler believes it will withstand anything the Allies can throw against it.

The recent storms in the English Channel have helped make the Germans feel secure. They are convinced that until the weather clears there is little chance the Allies will attack.

Moments after Eisenhower arrives at Southwick House, he is told by his chief forecaster that weather conditions are expected to improve—but only for a period of 36 hours. After that, the forecaster says, there will be another storm. Eisenhower consults with his advisers. Some are eager to go ahead with the invasion. Others recommend that the invasion be postponed.

It will take the Allied convoys a full day to reach the coast of France. If they are given the order to proceed, they will arrive there tomorrow, June 6,

> *Successful penetration of a defended beach is the most difficult operation in warfare.*
> —DWIGHT D. EISENHOWER

French civilians, such as this couple photographed in the town of Bayeux in 1944, carried on as best they could while Allied troops fought their way through German-occupied France. Many civilians were forced to take shelter as the violent struggle to liberate France went on around them.

just before dawn. Even if the weather does improve as promised, the seas in the Channel will still be rough. This will interfere with the accuracy of naval gunfire against the German defenses. It will also cause seasickness among the troops. More important, because the skies over the invasion area are expected to remain cloudy, flying conditions will be poor. The German ground forces will outnumber the Allied troops by a ratio of ten to one. Eisenhower knows that without effective air support, the Allied invasion is likely to fail.

On the other hand, it will be two full weeks before the tides in the Channel will be favorable again. The Germans are known to be developing new and lethal weapons—weapons that are not ready yet, but could be ready two weeks from now. The morale of the Allied troops has already reached its peak. Any further delay could destroy the fighting spirit of the thousands of young men who know they will have to storm the beaches of France in the face of withering German fire.

Eisenhower feels a deep and genuine affection for these men—and they for him. They admire his personal warmth and his honesty. As their supreme commander, he has done what any great leader must do: he has earned their respect.

At Southwick House it is now just after 4:00 A.M. The storm is already subsiding. The sky has begun to clear. One by one, Eisenhower's advisers fall silent. They know the final decision will have to be his. They also know the fate of the free world may

Field Marshal Erwin Rommel (1891–1944) was General Eisenhower's German adversary during the 1944 D-Day invasion. Nicknamed "The Desert Fox," Rommel had previously confronted Allied forces in the invasion of North Africa, also spearheaded by Eisenhower.

16

well depend on the soundness of his judgment. The invasion force—over 5,000 ships and landing craft, nearly 10,000 planes, and 156,000 men—is poised.

For several minutes Eisenhower paces the floor of the room, his large hands folded behind him, his brow knitted in concentration. To his advisers he seems terribly alone. Seldom in history has such an awesome decision rested on the shoulders of a single man. To make it, he relies on his instincts, his knowledge of the situation, and his experience as a commander in the field.

"Okay," he says finally. "Let's go."

Relieved to have the issue settled, his advisers break into a cheer. The order has been given. The Allied forces will invade the beaches of Normandy at dawn tomorrow—D-Day—June 6, 1944.

On June 6, 1944, American troops wade ashore at one of the five French beaches chosen as landing sites for the expedition against Nazi forces in Europe. Supported by 5,000 ships and nearly 10,000 aircraft, the thousands of British and American soldiers under Eisenhower's command met fierce German resistance.

2

The Will to Win

As supreme commander of the Allied Expeditionary Force, Eisenhower had already earned a place in history. Known to millions throughout the world by his nickname, "Ike," he would go on to hold many other top-level positions, and would cap his truly remarkable career by serving two full terms as president of the United States. He was 53 years old when he gave the order to launch the Normandy invasion.

Before serving in World War II, Eisenhower had spent most of his life as a staff officer in the United States Army. The country was at peace in those years and promotions were hard to get. Eisenhower expected to retire with a rank no higher than colonel. By the time he was 50 years old, he had had some interesting assignments, but none that were really exciting. (Much to his dismay, he had missed seeing combat in World War I.) Few people outside the military had ever heard his name.

No one—least of all Eisenhower himself—would ever have dreamed he was destined to become one of the most famous, powerful, and well-loved leaders of the Western world.

Dwight David Eisenhower was born on October 14, 1890, in a rented house in Denison, Texas. His parents were David and Ida Stover Eisenhower.

David and Ida Eisenhower's wedding picture. The couple met at Lane University, a Mennonite college in Kansas, and were married there on September 23, 1885, David Eisenhower's birthday.

Three-year-old Dwight D. Eisenhower (at right in first row) poses for a family portrait with three of his brothers. Eisenhower's parents belonged to a Christian religious sect, called the Mennonites, whose members lead plain, simple lives, and are opposed to military service.

Eisenhower was born in this modest house in Denison, Texas, on October 14, 1890. His parents moved there after the failure of a general store they ran in Kansas left the family bankrupt. The house is now a museum.

Dwight was the third in a family of six surviving sons.

David and Ida's ancestors came from Germany. They were Mennonites. This is a religious sect—still in existence—whose members believe in a plain and simple life style and are opposed to military service. Persecuted in Germany in the 18th century, many Mennonites came to the New World. The Eisenhowers and the Stovers were among them—though they did not know each other then. Farming people, they settled first in Pennsylvania, then moved on to the Midwest.

David and Ida met in 1884, when they were students at Lane University, a small school then run by the Mennonites in Lecompton, Kansas. David was a sophomore engineering student, tall, strong, with thick, dark hair and a manner that was both serious and shy. Ida, a newly arrived freshman who planned to study religion and music, was the outgoing one. She had a wonderful smile and beautiful brown hair, was optimistic about life, and loved to laugh.

David and Ida quickly fell in love and became engaged. They were married in September 1885. The world that lay ahead of them seemed full of excitement and opportunity. Their life together would be marked at first by financial disaster, and eventually, through the careers of their children, by extraordinary success.

David's father was a prosperous farmer in Abilene, Kansas, at that time. As a wedding gift, he gave David $2,000 in cash and a 160-acre farm. David, who had no interest in farming, promptly mortgaged the property and used the money to buy a general store in a nearby town. Two years later, in the midst of a severe agricultural depression, the store went bankrupt. David and Ida had lost everything. Humiliated by the failure of his venture, David left Abilene for Denison, Texas, where he took a job working for the railroad. Soon, Ida joined him there. There were already two boys in the family: Arthur and Edgar. Now, with Dwight's birth, there were three.

Before Dwight was one year old, David and Ida returned to Abilene. Their families had urged them to come back, promising them help if they did. One relative was foreman at the town's new creamery— a plant where butter and cheese were made. He saw to it that David was hired as a mechanic. David would work at the creamery for the rest of his life. Although he never made much money, he earned a reputation as a hard-working man who could always be counted on to pay his bills.

Abilene was a peaceful, rural community that served as a center for surrounding farms. Dwight and his family lived in a small rented cottage in the poor section of town for about six years. It was during this time that Dwight learned one of the first important lessons of his life.

When Dwight—or "Ike," as he was called by everyone except his mother—was about five years old, he visited his Aunt Minnie at her farm in Topeka. Little Ike was full of curiosity about the place and eager

Eisenhower (second from left, first row) poses with classmates at the Lincoln Elementary School in Abilene, Kansas, in 1900. Eisenhower later wrote of his days in primary school, "The darkness of the classrooms on a winter day and the monotonous hum of recitations . . . are my sole memories."

to see everything he could, but there was a gander in the back yard, and every time the boy would venture outside, the huge goose would come flapping and hissing after him, chasing him back into the house. Finally, his Uncle Luther gave Ike a broom and told him to go out and settle things with the gander once and for all.

The gander was about the same size as Ike, so the boy was not happy about having to confront it. But his uncle insisted, so Ike summoned up his courage and went out into the yard. As soon as he did, the gander started to come after him. Ike gave a yell, ran toward the bird, and gave it a whack on the backside with the broom.

From that moment on, Ike was boss of the back yard. Years later, he would say that from his experience with the gander he had learned a valuable lesson: Never deal with an adversary except from a position of strength.

By the time Ike was 10 years old, his family had moved to a small two-story house in the same poor section of town. The new property included a large barn and three acres of land, where the family could keep some livestock and raise hay for the animals and vegetables for themselves. In addition to his older brothers, Arthur and Edgar, Ike now had three younger brothers: Roy, Earl, and Milton.

The Eisenhowers had very little money. As the boys grew older, they were expected to pitch in to help the family survive. There were cows to milk, pigs to feed, horses to water, eggs to collect. Each boy had his own small garden where he could grow vegetables to sell to the neighbors. Ike grew sweet corn and cucumbers. "I have found out in later years we were very poor," he once said. "But the glory of America is that we didn't know it then. All we knew was that our parents—of great courage—could say to us: Opportunity is all about you. Reach out and take it." Whatever the financial hardships might have been, Ike always referred to his boyhood as "that golden time."

Ida, Ike's mother, was a major influence on his life. An intelligent, deeply religious yet tolerant woman, she urged each of her sons to go out and

Abilene provided both a healthy outdoor existence and a need to work. These same conditions were responsible for the existence of a society which, more nearly than any other I have encountered, eliminated prejudices based upon wealth, race, or creed, and maintained a standard of values that placed a premium upon integrity, decency, and a consideration for others.
—DWIGHT D. EISENHOWER
describing his
hometown in Kansas

compete in the world, and to be the very best person he could on any given day. She taught her sons the values of self-reliance, self-discipline, and honesty. Her manner was light-hearted, but for Ida life was chiefly a matter of survival. "Sink or swim," she would often say. "Survive or perish." In many important ways, Eisenhower's character and will to win were shaped by his mother's early counsel.

Ike's relationship with his father was also important, but very different. David Eisenhower was a strict authoritarian. He worked 12-hour shifts at the creamery, which kept him away from home through most of each day. He was devoted to his wife and family, but found it difficult to express his love. Usually quiet and reserved, he had an explosive temper that would erupt if one of his sons misbehaved. When this happened, he would cut a switch from a tree in the yard, grab the offending son by the collar, and whip him. This sort of punishment was more commonplace in those years than it is now. The boys feared their father, but they respected him for the hard work he did and for his devotion to their mother.

Ike, more than any of the other boys, had inherited his father's temper. When he was 10 years old,

The Eisenhower family in 1902. Dwight and his brothers Edgar, Earl, Arthur, and Roy are in the back row; David, Milton, and Ida are in front. The six young Eisenhowers all became professionals who achieved a measure of success.

Eisenhower (second from right, back row) with other players from the Abilene High School baseball team in 1908. A natural athlete, Eisenhower was highly competitive, but also a team player. Both qualities helped shape his leadership abilities.

this led to an incident that he would never forget. Arthur and Edgar had been given permission to go out "trick-or-treating" on Halloween. Ike desperately wanted to go with them, but his parents told him he was too young. He pleaded, but they refused to change their minds. When his brothers left, Ike went into a rage. He began beating his fists on an old apple tree in the yard, screaming out his fury. When he refused to stop, his father gave him a whipping and sent him to bed. An hour later, when his mother came into the room, he was still sobbing.

"Mother sat in the rocking chair by the bed and said nothing for a long time," Eisenhower would recall years later. "Then she began to talk about temper and controlling it."

She said hatred was a negative emotion that seldom accomplished anything, and often injured the person who expressed it. As Ike looked down at his hands, which were bruised and bleeding after his attack on the tree, he decided his mother was right. He had lost his temper, had expressed his hatred of others, and had only hurt himself.

"I have always looked back on that conversation," Eisenhower would remember, "as one of the most valuable moments of my life."

And he would spend the rest of his life doing his best to control his own explosive temper.

Young Eisenhower was full of energy, and always

wanted to be where the action was. He was a scrapper, and hardly a day went by when he did not get into a fight. At the start of his freshman year in high school, he slugged it out, in a battle now legendary in Abilene, with a boy named Wesley Merrifield. Merrifield was faster and stronger than Eisenhower, but Eisenhower, in spite of the punishment he was taking, refused to give up: the match was finally considered a draw.

In his early school days, except for spelling and math, Eisenhower was bored by his regular studies, but he loved to read military history. The stories of famous generals fascinated him. Soon he was reading nothing else. Worried that her son was paying too much attention to one subject, his mother locked his military books in a closet. The young man found the key and, whenever his mother was out of the house, would sneak out his books and go on with his reading.

During Eisenhower's boyhood years, an outdoorsman named Bob Davis also lived in Abilene. Davis, who was in his 50s, became a kind of hero to Eisenhower. They went on many expeditions together, along the Smoky Hill River. Davis taught Eisenhower how to hunt, fish, run a trap line, and cook over an open fire. Eisenhower thoroughly enjoyed these activities; he remained an avid outdoorsman throughout his life. Davis also taught Eisenhower how to play stud poker—and was thus responsible for Eisenhower's later fame as "the best stud poker player in the army."

In high school, Eisenhower got good grades without having to study very hard. Boys often did not finish high school in those days—many of them would drop out in order to go to work or to join the military. By the time Eisenhower graduated, 25 of

Abilene's postmaster, Phil W. Heath, owned and edited a local newspaper, the *Chronicle*, during Eisenhower's school days. In 1910 Heath composed a letter recommending Eisenhower as an applicant to the United States Military Academy at West Point, New York. He was accepted by the Academy in 1911.

the 34 students in his class were girls. Eisenhower tended to be shy around girls and was said to be a terrible dancer.

More than anything else during his school years, Eisenhower loved competitive sports, football and baseball in particular. He was on the light side, at 150 pounds, but he had good coordination and a strong desire to compete. He was a team player, confident of his own abilities, and quick to encourage the people around him. In the words of one of his biographers, "Ike's chief asset was his will to win."

In his freshman year, Eisenhower fell and cut his leg. The cut became infected, and the infection began to spread. The doctors finally said that, in order to save the young man's life, they would have to amputate his leg. Eisenhower said he would never let them do that, that he would rather die than lose his leg. Gradually the infection began to improve; the doctors had been wrong. Eisenhower missed two months of school (he had to repeat his freshman year), but he was able to play football and baseball again. And that had meant as much to him as being alive.

Eisenhower wanted to go to college, but there was too little money in the family. So Eisenhower got a job instead. He worked loading sheet metal into boxcars for a while, then took a job as night manager at the creamery. He worked seven nights a week, starting at 6:00 P.M., ending at 6:00 A.M.

During the summer of 1910, a friend named Everett Hazlett often dropped by while Eisenhower was working at the creamery. Hazlett, who was slightly younger than Eisenhower, was an intelligent boy and a good talker, but he was not aggressive and he did not like sports. This made him a target for the bullies in town. Eisenhower, who by now was one of the local sports heroes, stood up for his friend, and the bullies soon left Hazlett alone.

Eisenhower's main job at the creamery was to keep the furnace going. There was plenty of time to play poker in the boiler room and, when hunger struck, to fry some eggs or a chicken on a clean shovel over the coals. There was also plenty of time

All the Eisenhower boys—especially Dwight—were highly efficient, remarkably successful managers. They accepted the world as they found it and worked with the tools at hand to make it run better—not differently.
—STEPHEN AMBROSE
American historian

to talk. Hazlett had graduated from a military school in Wisconsin and had just received an appointment to the United States Naval Academy. He was very excited about his appointment and thought Eisenhower should seek an appointment too. Hazlett said it was one of the best educational opportunities available: it was free, and everyone who graduated was guaranteed a career in the navy. Most important—from Eisenhower's point of view—the football program was strong.

Eisenhower began a campaign to get an appointment. He asked all the important people he knew in Abilene if they would be willing to recommend him. They all said they would. By way of insurance, Eisenhower also applied for an appointment to the United States Military Academy at West Point. In October 1910 a competitive examination lasting two days was given in Topeka to applicants to the military academies. Eisenhower came in second, with an overall score of 87.5. One month later, he received an appointment to take the final entrance examination for West Point.

It had not been his first choice, but he was happy to have it. He went back to Abilene High School to take some extra courses and play another season of football. In January 1911 he took the West Point entrance examination and passed it easily. His brothers were extremely proud of him. His father, reserved by nature, had little to say. His mother was dismayed. Deeply religious, she was, in Eisenhower's words, "the most honest and sincere pacifist I ever knew." But she also believed each of her children had to be the master of his own fate. As opposed as she was to her son's choice of a military career, she did not stand in his way.

Eisenhower was 20 years old when he took a train for West Point in June 1911. He had added muscle during the last two years, stood five-feet, eleven-inches tall, was broad-shouldered and strong. His hair was brown, his eyes bright blue, his features distinguished by an appealing grin. He was confident in himself, and had reason to be. Full of possibilities, his life lay ahead of him. He was eager to go out and begin it.

Eisenhower was the most popular man in Abilene. . . . Young women found him charming because of his polite manner, honesty, and mature bearing. Young men liked him because he was such a good organizer, because of his enthusiasm for fun and games, and because he was a straight shooter, a fearsome competitor who nevertheless always played clean.
—STEPHEN AMBROSE
American historian

3

Eisenhower's Luck

My ambition in the Army was to make everybody I worked for regretful when I was ordered to other duty.
—DWIGHT D. EISENHOWER

Eisenhower arrived at West Point on June 14, 1911. That night, he was sworn in with the rest of his class as a cadet of the United States Military Academy. It was a moving experience for him. Suddenly, the American flag meant something very special to him—as it would for the rest of his life.

It is a tradition at West Point for the upperclassmen to make life miserable for the first-year "plebes." This tradition is called "hazing." (The expression comes from the Old French word *haser*, meaning "to irritate or annoy.") Hazing at West Point was worse in Eisenhower's time than it is today. Plebes were screamed at, ridiculed, forced to hold weights at arm's length, count the ants in an anthill, do hundreds of pushups, and run until they dropped. Their dormitory was called "Beast Barracks." If they missed a step while marching, they were immediately assigned to the "awkward squad." For the plebes, the entire experience was humiliating and painful. Some of them broke under the pressure and left the academy in tears.

Eisenhower accepted the hazing as something that had to be endured. He had the advantage of having worked at a hard job under a difficult boss.

In his dress uniform, Eisenhower with his future bride, Mary (Mamie) Doud (1896–1979), on the steps of St. Louis College in San Antonio, Texas. Eisenhower met Mamie in 1915 after he was assigned to nearby Fort Sam Houston. They were married the following year.

The great Native American athlete Jim Thorpe (1889–1953) won the decathlon and pentathlon during the 1912 Olympic games in Stockholm, Sweden. An outstanding player on the West Point football team, Eisenhower was injured in 1912 during a game against Jim Thorpe and the Carlisle Indian School.

He knew what it was like to be ordered around and to have unreasonable demands made of him. Also, he was a year or two older than most of his classmates, he was physically strong and, most important, he had a positive attitude.

Eisenhower was good on the rifle range, but not very good on the parade ground. As a result, he was assigned to the "awkward squad." He tried not to take such impositions too seriously, and managed to keep his sense of humor. Once, an upperclassman ordered Eisenhower and a fellow plebe to report to his room in "full dress coats." This referred to a full dress uniform—the army version of a tuxedo. Because the upperclassman had been particularly obnoxious in giving his order, the two plebes decided to take it literally; they showed up wearing *only* their coats. At the sight of the two otherwise naked plebes, the upperclassman went into a rage, while the rest of the cadets roared with laughter.

To become an officer in the United States Army was a distant goal for Eisenhower when he entered West Point. His immediate object was to get on the football team. At 154 pounds, he was too light to compete successfully during his first year. He spent the summer of 1912 undergoing a rigorous training program. By fall, his weight was up to 174 pounds, and he made the varsity.

Eisenhower's position was halfback. Quickly, his spirit and brilliant performances on the field caught the attention of sportswriters throughout the country. The *New York Times* described him as "one of the most promising backs in Eastern football." There was talk that he was destined to be an All-American. Then, playing against the great Jim Thorpe and the Carlisle Indian School, he injured his knee. He injured it again in a game against Tufts University, and then once more, this time very seriously, in a fall from a horse during a riding drill. The doctors told him he would never play football again. This time he knew their diagnosis was right and, for the first time in his life, he became deeply depressed. It was only the support of his classmates that kept him from dropping out of the academy.

Throughout his years at West Point, Eisenhower

> *When I get in a fight, I would rather have a courageous and honest man by my side than a whole boxcar full of pussyfooters.*
> —DWIGHT D. EISENHOWER

was an able but easygoing student. His academic performance showed little of the real motivation to excel that characterized his athletic performance. He had natural intelligence, and he counted on that, along with a little luck, to see him through. He did very well in English, but was only average in his other subjects. He enjoyed poker, and played a lot of it in his free time. Since smoking cigarettes was against the rules, Eisenhower began to smoke, probably as a way of asserting his independence. Demerits were given for all sorts of infractions of the rules. During his years at West Point, Eisenhower received numerous demerits, but they never bothered him. He had intended to enjoy his life at the academy, and he did.

There were 265 cadets in Eisenhower's class when he entered West Point. By the time he graduated, there were 164. Out of these, Eisenhower ranked 61st as a student. In matters of conduct, he ranked 125th.

On his graduation, Eisenhower was commissioned as a second lieutenant in the infantry. His

Eisenhower coaches the Tank Corps football team at Camp Meade, Maryland, in 1921. During World War I, Eisenhower had repeatedly asked for combat duty during the war, but was assigned to various posts in the South and Midwest, where he trained officer cadets and coached army football teams.

Preparing to defend against German attackers, American soldiers in the Meuse Valley man a trench abandoned by the enemy. During World War I, American troops distinguished themselves in the battle here in 1918. Germany surrendered shortly after Eisenhower had received orders to command a tank unit in Europe.

first assignment was to Fort Sam Houston, near San Antonio, Texas. He arrived there in September 1915. A month later, a major's wife introduced him to a young woman named Mary Geneva Doud. Mary, who was known as "Mamie," was 18 years old, vivacious and pretty. Eisenhower was immediately intrigued by what he called Mamie's "saucy" look; Mamie thought Eisenhower was "just about the handsomest male" she had ever seen. They began a whirlwind courtship. On Valentine's Day 1916, Eisenhower asked Mamie to marry him. She said yes. To make the engagement official, he gave her his West Point ring.

Mamie Doud came from a socially prominent family in Denver, Colorado. The Douds lived in a grand Victorian house, had servants, and sent their daughters to finishing schools. They liked Eisenhower at once and welcomed him into the family. Mr. and Mrs. Doud were more sophisticated people than Eisenhower was used to being around, and from them he would learn social graces that would help him throughout his career. As for Mamie, she was a friendly, strong-willed, very private person, unswervingly loyal to the people she loved.

The wedding took place on July 1, 1916, in the Douds' elegant Denver home. The groom wore his white, tropical dress uniform, and cut the wedding cake with his sword. Following a brief honeymoon in nearby Eldorado Springs, the young couple took the train to Abilene, where Mamie met Eisenhower's family. The Eisenhowers welcomed Mamie as warmly as the Douds had welcomed their son.

Less than a year after the young Eisenhowers returned from Abilene to Fort Sam Houston, the United States entered World War I, joining Britain, France, and Russia in their struggle against Germany. Eisenhower was eager to see combat, but all his requests for overseas duty were turned down. Instead, he was given numerous assignments in a variety of posts throughout the South and Midwest. He coached football, trained officer cadets, attended the army's first tank school, and was eventually put in command of the newly formed Tank Corps. This was a good assignment, but Eisenhower was not pleased with it. As always, he wanted to be where the action was, and the action was overseas.

The Eisenhowers' first child, a son named Doud Dwight, was born in San Antonio in 1917. For three years he was the center of his parents' lives—appealing, full of energy, quick to learn. Then, just before Christmas 1920, he caught scarlet fever; he died a week later. Years afterward, Eisenhower would write: "This was the greatest disappointment and disaster of my life."

Following the defeat of Germany in 1918, the United States began reducing the size of its army. Millions of soldiers and thousands of officers were discharged into civilian life. The "war to end all wars" had been fought. Most Americans wanted nothing more than to live in peace, secure within the borders of their own great land. By the time the demobilization was over, the United States Army would rank only 16th among all the armies of the world.

For the next 20 years, Eisenhower would be serving in this vastly reduced, peacetime army. He and Mamie had another child: John Sheldon Doud, born in 1922. They lived on bases in Colorado, Kansas,

Mamie Eisenhower holds 18-month-old John (b. 1922), the Eisenhowers' second child. John Sheldon Doud was born while Eisenhower was home on leave from an assignment in Panama. Doud Dwight (b. 1917), the couple's first child, died of scarlet fever in 1921, a week after Christmas. This tragic death greatly affected Eisenhower for many years.

Georgia, the District of Columbia, Panama, Paris, and the Philippines. Promotions came so slowly that Eisenhower held the rank of major for over 15 years. Many of his assignments were boring and frustrating, and there were times when his family and friends questioned his choice of career—as well as times when he must have questioned it himself.

Although there was much that annoyed Eisenhower about being in the peacetime army, there were things that pleased him as well. He had long been fascinated by military history, and, as a career officer, he had ample opportunity to pursue his study of the great generals and the major wars. He enjoyed the recreational and social life on the various bases where he served. He loved to travel, see new places, meet new people.

Major Eisenhower (seated on steps) and his family at a 1926 reunion held at his parents' home in Abilene, Kansas. On the front porch (from left to right) are his brothers Roy, Arthur, Earl, and Edgar. Milton, then an official in the United States Agricultural Department, stands behind David and Ida.

President Franklin Delano Roosevelt (1882–1945) delivers his first "Fireside Chat" radio broadcast in March 1933. Eisenhower greatly admired Roosevelt, who through these informal speeches brought hope and encouragement to Americans during the difficult years of the Depression and World War II.

During this long period—from 1920 to 1940—Eisenhower served under four of the most brilliant and powerful generals of his time: Fox Conner, John "Black Jack" Pershing, Douglas MacArthur, and George C. Marshall. These men—all of them demanding, and some of them extremely difficult to work for—saw great potential in Eisenhower and they helped him realize it. They all believed there was going to be another war and, when it came, they wanted the best of their young officers to be ready for it. Eisenhower had a lot to learn.

Eisenhower studied military history under Conner in Panama. He attended the Command and General Staff School—the toughest and most competitive school in the army—and graduated first in

Adolf Hitler, a gifted and charismatic speaker, addresses a Nazi party rally in Nuremberg in 1936. Under Nazi rule, mass rallies were used to stir powerful emotions and to instill dreams of nationalistic grandeur in their participants.

his class of 275. Under Pershing, he wrote a guide to the American battlefields in Europe. Assigned to the War Department (now the Department of Defense), he prepared detailed plans that would help the country mobilize if there should, indeed, be another war. He met businessmen and politicians, learning for the first time about what he would later call "the military-industrial complex." He served with MacArthur in the Philippines, helping the Filipinos prepare their defenses against the possibility of an attack by Japan.

Eisenhower gave his best to every assignment, no matter how tedious it might be. "My ambition in the Army," he once wrote, "was to make everybody I worked for regretful when I was ordered to other duty." As the years passed, Eisenhower's hard work and dedication began to pay off.

In September 1939 war broke out again in Europe. German armies stormed into Poland, and Britain and France, which were allied with Poland, declared war on Germany within days of the invasion. By this time, Eisenhower, who was now a lieutenant colonel, had earned a reputation as one of the best trained and most able staff officers in the United States Army. He was known for his attention to detail, his willingness to accept responsibility, his teamwork, and his integrity. He was also known for his personal charm. When people met Eisenhower, they liked him.

In 1940, as the United States began to prepare for the possibility that it might become involved in the European conflict, Eisenhower was put in command of an infantry battalion in the state of Washington. Nothing could have pleased him more. He loved being with the troops, helping to make good soldiers out of them, shaping their morale. Once,

Hilter's empire from 1938 to 1941. Areas shaded with diagonal lines show territories controlled by Germany or its allies during this three-year period. The nations then opposing Hitler, Great Britain and Greece, are represented by dotted areas. Areas shaded black represent Germany's borders at the close of World War I.

German soldiers battle the Soviet army in October 1941. Hitler astounded the world when he invaded the Soviet Union, breaking his nonaggression pact with Joseph Stalin (1879–1953). The invasion was a strategic blunder for Hitler, since the Soviets would later repel his attack and help to defeat Germany.

Yesterday, December 7, 1941— a date which will live in infamy—the United States of America was suddenly and deliberately attacked by naval and air forces of the Empire of Japan.
—FRANKLIN D. ROOSEVELT
speaking after the
Japanese surprise attack
on Pearl Harbor, Hawaii

feeling hungry while inspecting the camp kitchen, he grabbed a handful of raw hamburger, slapped a slice of raw onion on it and—much to the astonishment of the cook—ate it as he continued his inspection. The story quickly got around that Lieutenant Colonel Eisenhower was a pretty tough guy.

Eisenhower was 50 years old now. Much to his delight, his son John was about to enter West Point. Mamie, whose health had suffered during their tour in the Philippines, was feeling much better since they had returned to the United States. She was enjoying her role as wife of the battalion commander. She entertained well and was liked and respected by the troops.

It was a happy period for the family, marred only by the shadow of the war in Europe. In June 1941 Eisenhower was ordered to report to Fort Sam Houston, where he would serve as chief of staff under General Walter Krueger of the Third Army. Fort Sam

Houston was the base where Eisenhower and his wife had first met. A quarter of a century had passed since then, but they both felt as if they were coming home.

Their homecoming would be brief. Less than six months later, on December 7, 1941, the Japanese launched a surprise attack against the U. S. naval base at Pearl Harbor, in Hawaii. On December 11 Germany and Italy, which were committed by treaty to aiding Japan, declared war on the United States. The United States was at war. And Eisenhower, who had spent most of his life as an obscure officer in a peacetime army, was about to become one of the most famous and respected leaders of the 20th century.

American battleships burn after the Japanese surprise attack on Pearl Harbor, Hawaii on December 7, 1941. The Japanese, who had joined Hitler's Axis powers in 1940, tried to destroy the U.S. Pacific Fleet. The following day, the United States entered World War II by declaring war on Japan.

4

The Warrior

In addition to bombing Pearl Harbor, the Japanese had also bombed Clark Field near Manila in the Philippines. Five days after the attacks, General George C. Marshall, the army chief of staff, summoned Eisenhower, who had recently been promoted brigadier general, to Washington, D.C. Marshall was a crisp, cool, no-nonsense officer who, in a crisis atmosphere, was putting together a top-level staff. Marshall knew Eisenhower had spent time in the Philippines and was familiar with the situation there. At a meeting in Marshall's office at the War Department, Marshall sketched out the situation in the Far East. Then he looked at Eisenhower and said, "What do you think we should do?"

Eisenhower was taken aback. He asked Marshall if he could have a few hours to think it over. Marshall consented. That evening, Eisenhower gave Marshall a written statement. In it he said he believed the Philippines would eventually fall to the Japanese, whose forces were numerically superior to those of the Americans. He recommended that General Douglas MacArthur (the commander of the American forces in the Philippines) should hold out for as long as possible. This would give the United

The commander of the Allied forces in the Far East, American General Douglas Mac-Arthur (1880–1964), blamed Eisenhower for the crushing defeats suffered at Japanese hands in the Philippines in May 1942. Eisenhower did all he could, however, to provide MacArthur with supplies.

Victorious Japanese soldiers wave samurai swords and the Japanese flag to celebrate the surrender of a 36,000-man Allied garrison on the island of Bataan in the Philippines. Allied troops commanded by General Jonathan M. Wainwright (1883–1953) surrendered to the Japanese a month later at Corregidor.

POWs rest during the atrocious journey that became known as the "Bataan Death March." Tens of thousands of American and Filipino soldiers were forced to march 120 miles to a Japanese prison camp. Those who were too sick to continue were killed; more than half perished on the way.

States time to build a base of operations in Australia. Such a base, Eisenhower thought, would be essential if the Allies were to wage war successfully in the Pacific. Eisenhower was forceful and direct in presenting his ideas, and Marshall was impressed. He immediately put Eisenhower in charge of the Far Eastern Section of the War Plans Division.

The job was frustrating and painful. MacArthur's troops, quickly overwhelmed by the invading Japanese, were forced to retreat to the islands of Bataan and Corregidor. There, taking a final, desperate stand, they fought valiantly. However, with the Japanese controlling the seas, there was no practical way Eisenhower and the War Department could provide MacArthur with supplies and reinforcements. In March 1942 President Franklin D. Roosevelt, realizing that the situation was hopeless, ordered MacArthur to leave the Philippines for Australia. On April 9, the 36,000-man garrison on Bataan surrendered to the Japanese. A month later, the remaining troops, then fighting under General Jonathan M. Wainwright, surrendered on Corregidor.

MacArthur blamed Eisenhower and the General Staff for the loss of the Philippines. He said they had been halfhearted in their efforts and indifferent to the fate of his men. The charge angered Eisenhower, who, for five months at his desk in Washington, had worked 12- and 14-hour days, seven days a week, doing everything humanly possible to get help to MacArthur's beleaguered troops.

The battle for the Philippines was, of course, only one of many in a global war. Roosevelt and Marshall believed the way to end that war was to defeat the Germans on German soil, and, from Pearl Harbor on, they focused their attention on ways to accomplish that goal. Resources were still scarce. MacArthur's charge that the Philippines had been sacrificed to a larger cause was basically true. It was not true, however, that Eisenhower had lacked concern for MacArthur's men.

While MacArthur made his anger a matter of public record, Eisenhower did not. Aware of his own explosive temper, he had long since made a point of avoiding public controversy. In the privacy of his office, he might blow off steam in front of his secretary, or write an angry passage in his diary, but in public, if he could not find something good to say about someone, he would say nothing

In addition to the loss of the Philippines in the early months of the war, Eisenhower experienced a personal loss. In March 1942 his father died in Abilene. Eisenhower wrote in his diary, "I'm proud he was my father." His only regret, he wrote, was that "it was always so difficult to let him know the great depth of my affection for him."

Although the battle for the Philippines had been

> *No other war in history has so definitely lined up the forces of arbitrary oppression and dictatorship against those of human rights and individual liberty.*
> —DWIGHT D. EISENHOWER
> speaking about World War II

43

a losing cause, Eisenhower's handling of the situation had impressed Marshall. Eisenhower had more than lived up to his reputation as one of the Army's best staff officers. The problem was that Eisenhower did not want to be a staff officer; he wanted to command troops in the field. Having seen no combat in World War I, the idea he might miss it again was almost more than he could bear. Marshall sensed Eisenhower's dissatisfaction. In a moment of anger one day, he told Eisenhower not to expect a promotion. He said promotions were going to be given to officers in the field. "You're going to stay right here and fill your position," he told Eisenhower, "and that's that!"

This time, Eisenhower was unable to control his temper. "General," he said, "I'm interested in what you say, but I want you to know that I don't give a damn about your promotion plans . . . I came into this office from the field and I am trying to do my duty. I expect to do so as long as you want me here. If that locks me to a desk for the rest of the war, so be it!"

Then, having expressed his anger, and aware he was confronting the chief of staff, he broke into a grin. One week later, Marshall recommended that Eisenhower be promoted to major general. Eisenhower was never sure whether it was his outburst of temper or his quick control of it that had influenced Marshall's decision.

Eisenhower's style of positive, "can-do" leadership, combined with his great personal charm, had made him popular with the British during the first months after the United States entered the war. The British saw Eisenhower as someone with whom they could work. Marshall felt this too. As a result, in June 1942, he appointed Eisenhower commander of the European theater of operations. Before leaving for England to take up this assignment, Eisenhower spent a farewell weekend in Washington with his wife and son. It was the last time the three would be together until after the war.

Two weeks later, when Eisenhower arrived in England, he was given an elegant suite of rooms in London's most expensive hotel. A man of simple

Eisenhower has the power of drawing the hearts of men towards him as a magnet attracts the bits of metal.
—BERNARD MONTGOMERY
British general who served under Eisenhower in the European theater

tastes, he was appalled by the hotel's snobbish atmosphere and fancy trappings. He soon found a place in the country: a small house called "Telegraph Cottage" on the edge of a golf course in Kingston, Surrey. Secluded, but less than an hour's drive from the heart of London, it suited Eisenhower perfectly.

The American and British senior commanders had a common goal: the defeat of Germany. The question was how to do this, and when. Eisenhower and his staff believed the answer was to launch a cross-Channel invasion of France. They had already drawn up a plan, code-named "Roundup," for such an operation. The target date was April 1, 1943. The British, who had been driven out of France by the German armies in 1940, had many reservations about the wisdom of Roundup—but they had finally agreed to go along. In the summer of 1942, thousands of American troops were arriving in England to prepare for the proposed invasion. It was Eisenhower's job to supervise this buildup of forces.

Meanwhile the war was raging on the Eastern Front. Over a year had passed since the Germans attacked the Soviet Union with nearly 140 divisions in June 1941. Since then the Soviet armies had suffered millions of casualties. Joseph Stalin, the Soviet dictator, wanted help from the British and Americans. He was putting increasing pressure on the Allies to open up a second front by invading western Europe. He thought that Roundup, which was scheduled for the spring of 1943, should be brought forward. Stalin's forces were under terrible pressure, and the Soviet dictator and his generals wanted something done *now*, in the late summer or fall of 1942.

At Marshall's request, Eisenhower devised a plan for a smaller cross-Channel invasion, to be launched in September of 1942. The British thought the idea was too risky and flatly rejected it. Winston Churchill, the British prime minister, argued instead for an invasion of North Africa. Although this would do nothing to help the Soviets, and would probably only serve to increase their already considerable distrust of the Allies, Churchill had his way. The code name for the invasion of North Africa was to be "Torch."

> *Here is the answer which I will give to President Roosevelt: Put your confidence in us. . . . We shall not fail or falter; we shall not weaken or tire. Neither the sudden shock of battle, nor the long-drawn trials of vigilance and exertion will wear us down. Give us the tools and we will finish the job.*
> —WINSTON CHURCHILL in a radio address delivered on February 9, 1941, requesting material assistance from the United States

General George C. Marshall (1880–1959) possessed great patience and exceptional administrative abilities. It was Marshall who appointed Eisenhower to command all Allied forces in the European theater. After World War II Marshall was named secretary of state, and developed the Marshall Plan to rebuild postwar Europe.

Allied convoy on the North Atlantic. During World War II, the supplies vital to the war efforts of both sides were transported mainly over sea. Ships such as these supplied the Allied invasions of Africa and France.

Eisenhower—who believed the invasion was a serious mistake—was the Allied commander.

The major goal of Torch was to drive the Germans and Italians out of eastern and central North Africa by attacking them from the west. Eisenhower faced enormous problems in planning and carrying out this mission. He had to develop a team of British and American officers who would work together effectively day after day, under extremely tense conditions. These officers came from two different cultures. They had different accents, different slang expressions, different ways of carrying out their jobs. As commander of the expedition, Eisenhower had to bridge these differences. It was the first time in the history of the two nations that this had ever been tried.

The invasion of North Africa was a large-scale amphibious operation. More than 185,000 Allied troops would go ashore. Hundreds of miles separated the landing sites at Casablanca, Algiers, and Oran. Eisenhower and his staff had to work out landing schedules that were complicated by weather and tides, as well as ways to supply the troops once they were ashore. These were the logistics of Torch, and Eisenhower handled them with great expertise.

The political aspect of the invasion gave Eisenhower serious cause for concern. The French, who had colonized much of North Africa in the 19th century, had substantial military forces stationed throughout the region. There were several reasons why the Allied commanders could not be sure how these forces would react to the invasion.

Following its defeat by Germany in 1940, France had been divided into two administrative areas: the northern part of the country was under direct German military occupation, while the southern part was ruled by a collaborationist French government based in the city of Vichy. The Vichy government,

Admiral Jean-Louis Darlan (1881–1942) visits Hitler in Germany. A fascist who drafted anti-Semitic decrees, Darlan served in France's Vichy government, which collaborated with Hitler. To gain the Vichy government's support against the Germans, Eisenhower struck a deal with Darlan, angering many Americans.

which was sympathetic toward the Germans and hated the British for having withdrawn from France in 1940, considered itself the legitimate government of France. It had been recognized as such by the United States. Also, most of France's colonies had remained loyal to the Vichy regime.

Eisenhower had thus been given the job of invading the sovereign territory of a country with which the United States was not at war and which loathed his British allies. At the same time, Eisenhower was under pressure from General Charles de Gaulle, leader of the Free French forces. The Free French, who were aligned with the Allies and despised the Vichyites, were demanding that they be allowed to govern France's colonies in North Africa after the invasion.

Eisenhower knew that unless some agreement was reached with the Vichy French forces, they would resist the Allied invasion. As a military man, he had no patience with politics. He became so frustrated at one point in his relations with the French that he later said what he needed to solve the problem was "a damned good assassin!" He struck his first deal with a retired French general named Henri Giraud. As the Allied forces went ashore on November 8, 1942, Giraud went on the radio and urged the French troops not to resist. The French troops paid no attention to Giraud. Instead, they resisted the invasion on all three fronts: Casablanca, Algiers, and Oran.

Eisenhower was furious. His worst fears had been realized. British and American soldiers who had come to North Africa to fight the Germans were dying under French fire. Quickly, he decided to make a second deal, this time with Admiral Jean Darlan, who was deputy premier of Vichy France. It was one of the most controversial decisions Eisenhower ever made.

Darlan was a fascist. He had collaborated with the Nazis and hated both the British and the Jews. He represented everything the Allies were fighting against. Eisenhower chose Darlan because he thought he was the one French leader in North Africa who had enough influence to persuade the

French forces to stop firing on the Allies.

When the "Darlan deal" was reported by the Western press, there was such a firestorm of protest that Eisenhower almost lost his command. Although the "Darlan deal" would haunt Eisenhower for the rest of his life, it resulted in a cease-fire with the French forces, and probably saved the lives of thousands of Allied soldiers. It did not, however, save Darlan. A month later, he was assassinated by an anti-German Frenchman.

Many historians believe the Allied decision to invade North Africa in November 1942 was one of the biggest strategic blunders of the war. Eisenhower himself had been opposed to the operation. The American forces were inexperienced in desert warfare. Their principal adversary was Field Marshal Erwin Rommel, commander of Hitler's elite Afrika Korps. Known as "the Desert Fox," Rommel was a brilliant strategist who made the Allies pay dearly for every inch of ground they took.

Partly due to Eisenhower's own inexperience as a field commander, the North Africa campaign dragged on for six months. Nearly 11,000 Allied troops were killed, about 40,000 wounded, and over 20,000 captured. The campaign would soon lead Eisenhower and the Allies into long and bloody fighting in Sicily and Italy. And when these areas were finally secure, the Allied armies would still have the immense barrier of the Alps standing between them and German territory.

Soviet Premier Stalin, U.S. President Franklin D. Roosevelt, and British Prime Minister Winston Churchill (1874–1965) at Teheran, Iran, in December 1943. Stalin urged Roosevelt to help Soviet troops fight the Germans by attacking Hitler in Western Europe. Roosevelt named Eisenhower as commander of the offensive—the D-Day invasion.

It was during the campaigns in North Africa, Sicily, and Italy that Eisenhower gained valuable experience in planning and commanding large-scale amphibious assaults. He had weathered the storm of criticism over the "Darlan deal," and had been promoted four-star general. He had shown great intellectual and physical stamina, and was enormously popular with his troops. On December 7, 1943, President Roosevelt gave Eisenhower command of the long-awaited cross-Channel invasion of France.

The code name for that invasion had now been changed from Roundup to "Overlord." It would be the single most important operation of the war. By the time the invasion took place, Eisenhower would have 2.5 million men under his command.

Upon his return to London, Eisenhower was offered the use of a mansion for his personal quarters, decided it was too fancy, and went back to Telegraph Cottage, where he had lived before the North Africa campaign. His genuine preference for simple surroundings enhanced his popularity with the public and his troops.

Overlord would be the greatest air and sea invasion in the history of the world. From January through May 1944, Eisenhower worked day and

French Generals Henri Giraud (1879–1949) and Charles de Gaulle (1890–1970) of the Free French review troops in North Africa. Eisenhower first approached Giraud to obtain French cooperation for Allied invasion plans in North Africa.

night to ensure its success. He faced countless problems. One of them was security.

The German high command knew an invasion of France was coming, but they did not know where or when. To keep them off balance, the Allies executed a brilliant piece of deception, which was largely devised by the British military intelligence services. The code name for the plan was "Fortitude." It involved, among other things, giving the Germans the impression that an invasion army was being assembled in southeastern England, across from the French port of Calais. The plan made use of code intercepts, false radio messages, double agents, and simulated troop encampments.

Eisenhower helped bring about the success of Fortitude by placing General George S. Patton in command of 12 imaginary divisions across from Calais. Patton was the most charismatic general in the United States Army. He wore riding boots and brass-buttoned uniforms and he carried a pearl-handled revolver. He was also considered by the Germans to be the best general the Allies had.

With Patton in command of what appeared to be a major troop concentration across from Calais, the Germans naturally assumed Calais would be the target of the cross-Channel invasion. Quickly, they strengthened their defenses in that area. The Allied deception was so successful that the Germans maintained extra forces around Calais for many weeks after the actual landings had taken place further south on the Normandy coast.

As the hour of the invasion drew near, the weather became Eisenhower's main concern. Now operating out of his command trailer near Portsmouth, he had to deal with continuous forecasts of high winds, rough seas, and rain. On June 4 he recalled the ships that were already on their way to the beaches of France. On June 5, making the most difficult and crucial decision of his career—with the weather improving but still unpredictable—he gave the order for the invasion to proceed. "You are about to embark upon the Great Crusade," he said to his troops in his order of the day. "The eyes of the world are upon you."

Eisenhower and General Omar Bradley (1893–1981) inspect troop positions in Tunisia, North Africa. Eisenhower was personally opposed to the African campaign, "Operation Torch," yet he led the costly operation (11,000 Allied troops were killed), finally driving the Germans out of the region.

Eisenhower gives the 101st Airborne Division, called the "Screaming Eagles," a pep talk just before the paratroopers board planes headed for France. Although it was estimated that this unit would suffer a 70% casualty rate, the men were confident. The apprehensive Eisenhower heard a private shout "Look out, Hitler, here we come."

That evening, Eisenhower paid a visit to the troops of the 101st Airborne Division. These men, known as the "Screaming Eagles," were in full battle gear and about to leave for Normandy, where they would be dropped inland from the invasion beaches. Their mission would be to mine approach roads and demolish bridges, thereby slowing down German counterattacks. Eisenhower knew this mission was extremely hazardous, and it saddened him to realize that many of the young men who crowded around him would not live through the next 24 hours. Eisenhower not only had a special feeling for these men, but also for their parents. He knew what it was like to lose a son.

In the early hours of June 6, 1944, as Allied forces began storming five heavily fortified beaches along the Normandy coast of France, all Eisenhower could do was sit in his command trailer in England and wait to hear the results. He had given the crucial order. The rest would depend on luck, firepower, and on the fighting spirit of nearly 156,000 men. Eisenhower smoked one cigarette after another, tried to read a Western novel, paced the floor. These must have been the longest hours of his life.

The code names for the invasion beaches were "Utah," "Omaha," "Gold," "Juno," and "Sword." Except at Omaha, where German fire was extremely heavy, the landings went well. Eisenhower surveyed the beaches the next day from the deck of a British ship. On June 12, he went ashore. The invasion had been a tremendous success. Within three weeks, more than 1 million Allied troops were on French soil. The war was not over, but the tide had definitely turned.

Eisenhower was delighted. He became even happier when his son John (who had graduated from West Point on the day of the invasion) arrived in England on June 13, intending to spend his two-week graduation leave there. It had been two years since Eisenhower had seen him. John's orders were to report for infantry-officer training at Fort Benning, Georgia, at the end of June. He asked his father to use his influence to have these orders changed to a combat assignment. Eisenhower, not

Eisenhower conferring with British Field Marshal Bernard L. Montgomery (1887–1976) on July 26, 1944. Eisenhower pressured Montgomery to cooperate on a coordinated Allied attack. Montgomery disagreed at first, but finally he ordered the British forces to "accept any casualties and to step on the gas."

wanting to show favoritism to his son—and afraid of Mamie's reaction to such a move—refused.

Despite the fact that the Allied Expeditionary Force was now firmly established on French soil, Eisenhower's problems as supreme commander were only just beginning. Eleven months of bitter fighting still lay ahead. During this difficult period, Eisenhower faced constant daily tests of his ability to lead. Some of his best officers, particularly Patton and British General Bernard Montgomery, were brilliant but also arrogant and egotistical. As the Allies began to drive the Germans out of France and Belgium, these generals frequently disagreed with Eisenhower about strategy. They constantly hounded him for more supplies, more troops, more opportunities to outshine one another. In addition, there were the continual problems of bad weather, fuel shortages, insufficient infantry forces, and the ever-present threat of German counterattack. In addition to these pressing matters, Eisenhower had to deal with the often conflicting desires of the two most powerful political leaders in the Western world: Roosevelt and Churchill. Complicating things still further were the often contradictory demands of de Gaulle.

Under heavy German rifle and machine gun fire, Allied infantrymen advance toward Periers, France. After the Allies stormed the Normandy beaches, it took almost a year of intense fighting against vicious counterattacks before Eisenhower secured Germany's surrender on May 7, 1945.

General George S. Patton (1885–1945), nicknamed "Old Blood and Guts," was a flamboyant figure who carried an ivory-handled revolver. Patton, who was much respected by enemy officers, helped trick the Germans into thinking the Allied invasion of France would take place at Calais rather than Normandy.

It is hard to imagine a more difficult or stressful job than the one Eisenhower had as supreme commander of the Allied Expeditionary Force. He once said he felt "like a flea on a hot griddle," and on another occasion said he seemed "to live on a network of high tension wires."

In spite of the job's many difficulties, Eisenhower displayed great energy and determination. He met with the world's leaders in London and Versailles, France, visited his troops on the battlefield, boosted the morale of his officers, and even surveyed the fighting from the air, flying over enemy lines in a fighter plane.

There were times when his health suffered, times when he made mistakes in strategy, times when he was accused of being indecisive and of giving his generals too much independence. But looking back on those crucial months of World War II, it seems clear that Eisenhower was right far more often than he was wrong, that he did more than any other leader to preserve the harmony among the Allies, and that he never lost sight of his original orders from the combined chiefs of staff: "You will enter the continent of Europe and, in conjunction with the other Allied nations, undertake operations aimed at the heart of Germany and the destruction of her armed forces."

In December 1944, under Eisenhower's direct command, the Allies turned back what would prove to have been the Germans' last counteroffensive on the Western Front. This desperate engagement became known as the Battle of the Bulge. The "bulge" was the balloon-like indentation created in the Allied lines when 20 German divisions crashed through them along a 50-mile front in Belgium.

With the Soviets advancing steadily from the east, and the Allies from the west, the fate of Hitler's Germany was sealed. Churchill and others urged Eisenhower to race the Soviets to Berlin, but he refused. The great powers—the United States, Great Britain, and the Soviet Union—meeting at the Soviet city of Yalta in February 1945, had already agreed on the postwar division of Germany. Its capital, Berlin, was well inside the Soviet zone. The

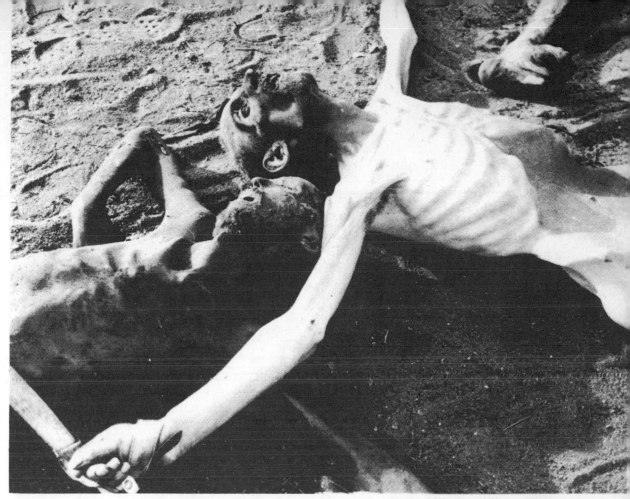

nearest Allied armies were still over 200 miles from Berlin; the nearest Soviet armies were less than 35 miles from the city. To try and beat the Soviets to Berlin did not make sense to Eisenhower. In order to create a lasting peace, Eisenhower believed, it was essential to establish a relationship with the Soviets that would be based on mutual trust and good will. Some historians believe Eisenhower was extremely naive in this matter; others think he made the wisest decision possible at the time.

In early 1945 Eisenhower visited a German concentration camp—one of many such camps that Hitler had ordered set up to carry out his plan to exterminate the Jews of Europe. Eisenhower had heard about these ghastly "death factories" but he was still shocked by what he saw. In a letter to his wife he said: "I never dreamed that such cruelty,

When Allied soldiers liberated Hitler's concentration camps, they discovered the atrocities of the Holocaust. Eisenhower, after visiting one of the "death factories" to witness the horrors firsthand, wrote to his wife, Mamie, "I never dreamed that such cruelty, bestiality, and savagery could really exist in this world!"

57

Survivors of the atomic bomb blast that destroyed the Japanese city of Hiroshima, on August 6, 1945. President Harry Truman (1884–1972) ordered a second bomb dropped on Nagasaki, three days later. Approximately 100,000 people were killed immediately—a figure that doubled when people succumbed to radiation sickness.

I'm old—my days of romance may be all behind me—but I swear I think I miss you more and love you more than I ever did.
—DWIGHT D. EISENHOWER
writing from England to
his wife, Mamie,
during World War II

bestiality, and savagery could really exist in this world!"

On April 30, 1945, with the war in Europe drawing to a close, Hitler committed suicide at his command bunker in Berlin. One week later, on May 7, 1945, Eisenhower accepted the unconditional surrender of General Alfred Jodl, the German chief of staff. These events marked the end of Hitler's monstrous tyranny.

Tremendously popular after the fall of Germany, Eisenhower was the guest of honor at victory celebrations in many of Europe's capitals. When he returned to the United States for a brief visit in June 1945, he was greeted by a ticker-tape parade in New York City, hailed by the press, and cheered by millions. The demands on his time were so great that he had little to spend with Mamie and John. Mamie, especially, was upset by this.

There had been rumors throughout the war that Eisenhower had fallen in love with Kay Summersby, a beautiful Irish woman who had served as his chauffeur and personal assistant. Eisenhower had spent much of his time with Summersby, both on and off duty, and though he always insisted that their relationship was strictly professional, many of those close to them thought otherwise. In 1976, seven years after Eisenhower's death and just before her own, Summersby wrote a best-selling book, *Past Forgetting: My Love Affair with Dwight D. Eisenhower.* Deeply distressed, Mamie then authorized the publication of her husband's hundreds of wartime letters to her. Entitled *Letters to Mamie*, the book offered convincing proof that Eisenhower's love for his wife had remained deep and constant, no matter what temporary upheavals the war had created in his personal life.

Although the Germans had finally surrendered, the war against Japan raged on in the Pacific. Roosevelt had died in April. His vice-president, Harry S. Truman, had succeeded him, and was now commander in chief. Eisenhower believed the Japanese were already beaten, and he was opposed to using the newly developed atomic bomb against them. Truman disagreed. The first bomb was dropped on Hiroshima, Japan, on August 6, 1945; the second on Nagasaki on August 9, 1945. With the surrender of the Japanese one week later, World War II was over at last. Fifty million people had died in the course of the conflict.

For millions of the survivors, one man more than any other seemed to represent the brightest hope for the future.

His name was Dwight D. Eisenhower.

> *You have completed your mission with the greatest victory in the history of warfare.*
> —GEORGE C. MARSHALL
> American general who, in 1942, appointed Eisenhower to command the European theater of operations

General Douglas MacArthur adds his signature to the agreement representing Japan's unconditional surrender, aboard the battleship U.S.S. Missouri in Tokyo Harbor on September 2, 1945. About 50 million people, 14 million of whom were military personnel, died in World War II.

5

Farm Boy to President

Eisenhower had risen to the highest military rank—five-star general—by the time the war ended. He was now one of the most popular and respected leaders in the Western world. Democrats and Republicans alike urged him to run for the presidency of the United States. Eisenhower said he was not interested, that he wanted "nothing to do with politics," and that he was just a "Kansas farmer boy" who had done his duty in the war. He declared that all he wanted to do now was finish his tour of duty, then retire with Mamie to some quiet place in the country where he could sit by a stream and fish.

In November 1945 Truman appointed Eisenhower chief of staff of the army, a position he held for over two years. During this time, he gave numerous speeches around the country and became friends with many powerful businessmen and politicians. These people kept pressuring him to seek the presidency in 1948. The polls at the time showed that he was the first choice among both Democrats and Republicans. Truman himself thought Eisenhower would be unbeatable. But Eisenhower continued to say no.

There were significant changes in Eisenhower's family during these early postwar years. He had al-

General Eisenhower was appointed commander of the North Atlantic Treaty Organization (NATO) forces in 1949. When NATO was established, its twelve member nations formed a policy of mutual defense. Eisenhower proved himself to be an effective negotiator by reconciling differences among America's allies in order to strengthen the alliance.

A United Nations patrol scrambles over snow-covered terrain in South Korea. As World War II neared its conclusion in 1945, the U.N. was established as an international peacekeeping organization. When the North Korean communists invaded South Korea in 1950, the U.N. intervened by sending an international fighting force into the region.

On its way to the battlefront in South Korea, an American tank passes a Korean farmer leading his ox. Contrary to Eisenhower's hopes for peace, the Soviets installed a communist regime in North Korea and backed its invasion of South Korea.

ready lost his father and, at about the same time, his younger brother Roy. Now, in September 1946, his mother, Ida, died peacefully in her sleep at the age of 84. Her five surviving sons gathered for her funeral at the family home in Abilene. Each had achieved a measure of success: Arthur as a banker, Edgar as a lawyer, Earl as a public-relations man, Milton as an educator and as an adviser to his famous brother. Roy had been a pharmacist. The sons of David and Ida Eisenhower had led full and in some cases extraordinary lives.

There was also a happy change in the Eisenhower family at this time. In June 1947 John married Barbara Thompson, the daughter of an army colonel. His parents were delighted.

On February 7, 1948, Eisenhower retired from the army. He wrote a book, *Crusade in Europe*, which became an instant best seller. He served for a while as president of Columbia University in New York, then as commander of the newly formed North Atlantic Treaty Organization (NATO) forces in Europe. NATO, which was established in 1949, began with 12 countries: the United States, Canada, Great Britain, France, Belgium, the Netherlands, Denmark, Norway, Iceland, Luxembourg, Italy, and Portugal.

These countries had agreed on a policy of mutual defense: they would consider an attack on any one of them as an attack on all of them. For the rest of his life, Eisenhower would remain one of NATO's strongest supporters.

Eisenhower's popularity with the public and the press seemed to grow with each passing year. His new friends, many of them millionaires, continued to urge him to run for the presidency. Top-level Republicans told him he was the only candidate who could unify their party and go on to beat the Democrats in 1952. Groups called "Citizens for Eisenhower" sprang up around the country. Countless rallies were held. Thousands of people chanted the slogan *"We want Ike! We want Ike! We want Ike!"*

In February 1952, touched by this outpouring of support, and with his tour as NATO commander coming to an end, Eisenhower finally agreed to run for president of the United States.

Eisenhower ran as a moderate Republican. His opponent in the primary election was Robert Taft, son of former President William Howard Taft. Robert

> *The necessary and wise subordination of the military to civil power will be best sustained when lifelong professional soldiers abstain from seeking high political office.*
> —DWIGHT D. EISENHOWER in a 1948 letter to a friend, insisting that he would not accept a presidential nomination

On returning to the United States from World War II battlefields in Africa and Europe, Eisenhower found that he had become a national hero. In 1948 the general authored a book entitled *Crusade in Europe*. Soon citizen groups began calling on Eisenhower to run for the presidency.

A child in Seoul, South Korea, keeps warm by wearing a pair of American combat boots and wrapping himself in a poster welcoming President-elect Eisenhower to the war-ravaged nation. Three weeks after he won the 1952 election, the former general traveled to Korea, and perceived the conflict there as unwinnable.

Taft was a champion of the "Old Guard" conservative wing of the Republican party. Eisenhower was the popular favorite, but Taft had the political edge. They battled each other all the way to the Republican National Convention in July; and it was only after some skillful back-room maneuvering on the part of Eisenhower's supporters that he finally won the nomination. The vice-presidential nominee was a young senator from California named Richard M. Nixon.

As Eisenhower began his campaign for the presidency, the country was once again at war—this time as part of the United Nations forces fighting in Korea. (The United Nations had been established in 1945 as an international organization of the world's states dedicated to cooperation and peacekeeping.) The North Korean communists had invaded South Korea in June 1950. To millions of people in the Western democracies, the invasion was a clear example of communist aggression; they were sure the source of that aggression was the Soviet Union.

At the end of World War II, Eisenhower had hoped the alliance between the United States and the Soviet Union could be preserved. He had formed a warm friendship with Georgi Zhukov, one of the Soviet Union's most senior generals. Zhukov and Eisenhower had liked each other from the moment they met. They shared a mutual respect and had no trouble getting along. Eisenhower believed that if he and Zhukov could be friends, so could the United States and the Soviet Union.

In spite of Eisenhower's hopes, relations between the two countries had deteriorated during the first years of the postwar period. The Soviets had refused to release their grip on the eastern European countries that they had liberated from the Germans. They had developed their own atomic bomb and had supported the invasion of South Korea. They appeared to stand at the head of a unified communist movement that had as its ultimate goal the domination of the entire world.

As the 1952 election approached, anticommunism was on the rise in the United States. Fear of traitors and spies was widespread. In 1951 two American citizens, Ethel and Julius Rosenberg, were convicted of passing U.S. atomic secrets to the Soviet Union. Sentenced to death, the Rosenbergs appealed in vain to the U.S. Supreme Court. Following the rejection of their subsequent appeal to President Truman, the Rosenbergs' execution was scheduled for June 1953.

Most Americans sincerely believed that the Soviet Union was a threat to them and to democracies everywhere. Their basic distrust, however, was whipped into a state of near-hysteria by a handful of politicians who used the "Red Menace" to gain publicity for themselves. The most prominent of these opportunists was Joseph McCarthy, a Republican senator from Wisconsin.

McCarthy accused the Democrats of "20 years of treason." He said President Roosevelt and the Democrats had "conspired" to deliver eastern Europe to the Soviets at the Yalta Conference in 1945. He accused Truman and the Democrats of having allowed China to be taken over by communists in 1949, and said the U.S. government, particularly the State Department, was riddled with communists, communist sympathizers, and other subversives.

McCarthy never hesitated to make extremely damaging accusations for which he had no proof. He destroyed the reputations of countless innocent people by labeling them "card-carrying communists." Although few of his assertions had any factual basis, they were made during a time when the public was already fearful about communism, and millions of Americans— for a while— believed everything he said.

Eisenhower had no use for McCarthy or his methods, but he had long since decided that the Soviet Union represented a clear and crucial danger to the West. "This is not just a casual argument against slightly different philosophies," he had said while he was president of Columbia University. "This is a war of light against darkness, freedom against slavery, Godliness against atheism."

Eisenhower's Democratic opponent in the 1952 presidential campaign was Governor Adlai E. Ste-

We face a hostile ideology, global in scope, atheistic in character, ruthless in purpose, and insidious in method.
—DWIGHT D. EISENHOWER
speaking about the
Soviet Union

venson II of Illinois. Stevenson was, in many important respects, an unlikely candidate for president of the United States. He was relatively unknown, had few political acquaintances, and had only limited financial backing. Eisenhower, on the other hand, was a popular national figure, a symbol of American freedom who had the overwhelming support not only of his party but of the press and the public. Stevenson, a wry, witty, and somewhat rumpled intellectual, seemed no match for the dashing military hero.

Stevenson, whose father served as secretary of state of Illinois and whose grandfather had been vice-president of the United States under Grover Cleveland, was an exceptional orator. His literate, carefully crafted speeches were often too sophisticated to appeal to the American public, but he exuded an air of confidence that was disconcerting to the Eisenhower camp.

The campaign was one of the most bitterly contested of modern times. Nixon repeatedly accused the Democrats of harboring crooks and communists in Washington. Then Nixon himself was accused by the Democrats of having a secret, and perhaps illegal, campaign fund. Eisenhower urged Nixon to take his case to the American people. Nixon went on television and successfully defended himself with his now famous "Checkers" speech. He said there certainly was a "Nixon fund," but that its money—which was handled by an independent attorney—was used legitimately, for "exposing communism." Nixon then made a tongue-in-cheek confession: he had indeed received a personal political contribution. It was a cocker spaniel named Checkers; his little girls loved the puppy, he said, and "we're gonna keep it!" In the meantime, Eisenhower's publicists were portraying Stevenson as indecisive (he had hesitated in seeking the nomination until the very last minute), and Eisenhower was being criticized by the Democrats for not denouncing McCarthy.

Eisenhower believed that the support of McCarthy and the Republican Old Guard was essential to his winning the election. Consequently, when Mc-

If I talk over the people's head, Ike must be talking under their feet.

—ADLAI STEVENSON II
Democratic governor of Illinois who lost to Eisenhower in the 1952 and 1956 U.S. presidential elections

The General has dedicated himself so many times, he must feel like the cornerstone of a public building.

—ADLAI STEVENSON II

Carthy viciously attacked Eisenhower's former boss, General George C. Marshall, Eisenhower failed to come to his defense for fear of losing that support. Eisenhower privately remarked that since McCarthy had just won a primary by more than 100,000 votes, to condemn him could mean alienating a large segment of the voting population. Many of Eisenhower's supporters, however, were dismayed because, whatever his reasons, he would neither stand up for Marshall nor disown McCarthy.

In 1952, when Eisenhower ran for the presidency, he was 61 years old—too old, said the Democrats, for the job. Eisenhower quickly proved them wrong. During the physically strenuous, two-month campaign, Eisenhower traveled over 50,000 miles through 45 states. He did most of his traveling on board his campaign train, called the "Look Ahead, Neighbor." At hundreds of whistle-stops around the country, with a smiling Mamie at his side, Eisenhower gave brief speeches from the rear platform of

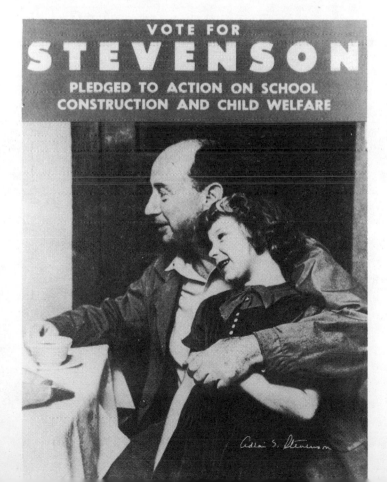

Adlai Stevenson II (1900–1965), pictured in this 1956 campaign poster, ran twice for president of the United States. Eisenhower's popular appeal as a war hero proved more attractive to Americans than Stevenson's intellectual image. In 1952 Eisenhower won the presidency by an unprecedented landslide. He again defeated Stevenson in 1956.

the train. He promised the crowds that, if elected, he would bring them four years of prosperity and peace. Then, as the train pulled away, he would flash his famous grin and show the V-for-Victory sign.

The crowds loved "Ike." To them he was not only a famous general, he was a decent, trustworthy human being. As the campaign drew to a close, he announced that if he were elected he would go to Korea to see what could be done about ending the war. This was all the American people needed to hear. When the votes were counted, Eisenhower and Nixon had won a landslide victory.

Eisenhower was true to his word. Three weeks after the election, he went to Korea. He wasted no time with the politicians and generals who were eager to be seen with the president-elect. Instead, he went directly to the front lines. The ground was covered with snow, the temperatures freezing. He talked with the soldiers, ate with them, observed an artillery battle, and was flown on a reconnaissance mission over the lines. At once, he saw the war for what it had become: a bloody and hopeless stalemate between two armies, neither of which had sufficient strength to win.

Eisenhower waves to delegates at the 1952 Republican convention after winning his party's presidential nomination on the first ballot. During the campaign his running mate Richard M. Nixon (b. 1913) concentrated on attacking the Democrats while candidate Eisenhower took the "high road," and promised peace and prosperity.

On January 20, 1953, Eisenhower was inaugurated as the 34th president of the United States. As soon as he took office, he began to work toward securing peace in Korea. Many members of the Republican Old Guard, including his former boss, General Douglas MacArthur, urged him to use the atomic bomb to end the conflict. Eisenhower was totally opposed to this. He did not believe the interests of the United States would be well served by resorting once again to that terrifying weapon. Eisenhower realized that using the atomic bomb could lead to a catastrophic war with China and the Soviet Union.

Several of Eisenhower's advisers, including John Foster Dulles, his ultra-conservative secretary of state, urged the president to go for an all-out victory with conventional forces. Eisenhower never believed the country could afford or would support such an effort. Instead, he used the power of his office to establish a firm policy regarding the handling of the Korean War. He issued a warning to the enemy that he would widen the conflict if he believed that he had no alternative but to do so. Eisenhower then used his own great personal prestige to bring about a negotiated peace. It did not come easily. For six months, while the peace talks dragged on, American soldiers continued to die in the stalemated war. Eisenhower's own son John was an officer in the battle zone.

Finally, in July 1953, the North Korean communists and the United Nations forces signed a truce at Panmunjom, a small town on the border between South Korea and North Korea. Eisenhower was delighted. Ending the Korean War, which had cost the lives of some 34,000 Americans, was one of the great achievements of his career.

Less than a week before Eisenhower was elected president, the United States had tested its first hydrogen bomb, at the tiny North Pacific island of Eniwetok. This bomb was 150 times more powerful than the atomic bomb that had been dropped on Hiroshima to end World War II. The Soviets were also testing nuclear weapons. By the time Eisenhower took office, the world's most powerful nations

Eisenhower reacts to the news that President Harry S. Truman has fired General MacArthur, commander of the U.N. military forces in Korea. MacArthur had repeatedly criticized Truman's policies in the region, and urged him to expand the war into mainland China. Then commander of NATO under Truman, Eisenhower kept silent about Truman's decision.

American soldiers celebrate the cease-fire in Korea. The U.N. had demonstrated its willingness to become actively involved in military disputes, and the United States had shown that it would sacrifice American lives to check communist aggression.

were frantically trying to outdo one another in the production of such weapons. Eisenhower believed that the arms race, if left unchecked, could jeopardize the future of mankind.

As president, Eisenhower wanted more than anything else to achieve a lasting peace—not only in Korea but throughout the world. On December 8, 1953, he addressed the General Assembly of the United Nations. He said the United States already had a stockpile of atomic weaponry that had more explosive power than all the bombs and shells that had been expended in World War II. He pointed out that the Soviets were building a similar arsenal, and said that the time had come for the two superpowers to end the arms race. He announced that the United States was prepared to discuss disarmament with the Soviet Union, and he proposed the creation of an International Atomic Energy Agency that would explore peaceful uses of nuclear technology.

One of Eisenhower's biographers, Stephen E. Ambrose, refers to Eisenhower's "Atoms for Peace" proposal as "the most generous and the most serious offer on controlling the arms race ever made by an American president." The Soviets, however, were not impressed. They felt the proposal was simply a way for the United States to maintain its own nuclear superiority. They also strongly opposed on-site inspections as a means of verifying progress on disarmament. The Soviets rejected Eisenhower's proposal, and the arms race continued.

Eisenhower was now faced with the hard realities of the Cold War. Many Americans, particularly the conservative wing of the Republican Party, continued to believe that isolationism—a policy that would keep the United States out of foreign alliances—was the wisest course for the country to follow. They envisaged a "Fortress America" secure behind its nuclear shield, living safely apart from the rest of the world.

Eisenhower thought the "Fortress America" idea was nonsense. He believed the United States' interests throughout the world were vital to the country's survival, and that access to international markets and raw materials was essential. Communism, he believed, was aggressive by its very nature and, if left unchallenged, would spread like a cancer. Nation after nation, he feared, particularly in the developing Third World, would fall under Soviet domination.

In military matters, Eisenhower was a practical man. He knew any nuclear war between the United

British Field Marshal Montgomery, Eisenhower, Soviet Marshal Georgi Zhukov (1896–1974), and Deputy British Commander of the Allied Expeditionary Force Arthur Tedder (1890–1967) celebrate the Allied victory in World War II. His excellent relations with Zhukov encouraged Eisenhower's hopes for cooperation between the Soviet Union and the United States.

Senator Joseph R. McCarthy (1908–1957) whose Senate career was devoted to hunting alleged communists, confers with his chief counsel, Roy Cohn (right). President Eisenhower disappointed some supporters by refusing publicly to attack McCarthy and his methods. He finally used "executive privilege" to prevent McCarthy from questioning members of the White House staff in 1954.

States and the Soviet Union would annihilate both countries. Korea had convinced him that conventional wars were no longer winnable. This left only one way, he believed, to combat Soviet aggression: "covert," or undercover, activities by agents of the Central Intelligence Agency (CIA).

Covert operations against communist governments had been authorized by the Truman administration as early as 1950. Eisenhower began to increase these activities soon after he took office. The first operation he authorized was against Mohammed Mossadegh, the prime minister of Iran.

Mossadegh had recently nationalized Britain's Iranian oil fields and refineries. The British had responded with an economic blockade of Iranian oil. Mossadegh appealed to Eisenhower for help. Eisenhower refused. According to his intelligence reports, Mossadegh had the support of the Soviet Union. In a top-secret operation, approved by Eisenhower himself, agents of the CIA launched a successful coup against Mossadegh, and arranged for the return to power of Mohammed Reza Pahlavi, the *shah*, or king, of Iran, who was pro-British and anticommunist. Eisenhower, who publicly denied any prior knowledge of the coup, was more than satisfied with its results.

Eisenhower would eventually authorize similar covert operations in Cuba, Central America, Asia, Africa, and the Mideast. Top secret and classified, these clandestine activities—and Eisenhower's role in them—have only recently become known to the American people. Some have faulted Eisenhower for stooping in his foreign policy to the very tactics he despised in the communists. Others have said he was simply being realistic: that to fight fire with fire was the only choice he had.

Vietnam, a country in Southeast Asia, was another trouble spot Eisenhower had to face soon after he became president. The French, who had been a colonial power in the region since the mid-19th century, had been fighting a war against the communist Vietnamese and their leader, Ho Chi Minh, since 1946. By 1954, the war was going badly for the French. For years, the United States had been supporting the French with money to carry on the war. Now, as their situation began to grow desperate, the French wanted the United States to give them bomber planes and aircraft mechanics as well as cash. With some reluctance, Eisenhower agreed.

From Eisenhower's point of view, it was essential to American economic and political interests that Vietnam should not fall to the communists. He believed that, were it to do so, the other nations of Southeast Asia would fall as well—not only the neighboring countries of Laos and Cambodia, but

Don't join the book burners. Don't think you are going to conceal faults by concealing evidence that they ever existed.
—DWIGHT D. EISENHOWER
speaking at
Dartmouth College in
Hanover, New Hampshire,
June 14, 1953

Eisenhower's running mate Richard Nixon delivers his televised "Checkers" speech. Nixon claimed that the only "secret" contribution he and his family had received was a puppy named Checkers. His $18,000 "expense fund," he said, was used to fight communism.

Thailand, Malaysia, Indonesia, and perhaps eventually Japan, Taiwan (then known as Formosa), the Philippines, Australia, and New Zealand. This was Eisenhower's "falling domino" theory, which was endorsed by most of his top advisers.

Just as they had with Korea, many of these advisers urged Eisenhower to authorize the use of the atomic bomb to save the French from defeat. Once again, he refused. He also rejected the idea of sending American soldiers into the Vietnam conflict. The jungles of Indochina, he warned, "would absorb our troops by divisions."

In the absence of direct U.S. intervention, the French were forced to surrender. On July 21, 1954, accords were signed in Geneva, Switzerland, between the French and the victorious forces of Ho Chi Minh. In these agreements, the country of Vietnam was temporarily divided into two parts at the 17th parallel. Ho Chi Minh had already taken firm control of the north and, as a popular nationalist leader, had considerable support in the south. The agreements guaranteed that nationwide elections would be held within two years.

Recognizing that Ho Chi Minh and the communists would almost certainly win these elections, Eisenhower refused to sign the Geneva accords. Instead, he put together the Southeast Asia Treaty Organization (SEATO). This organization, based on the NATO model, consisted of eight countries: the United States, Great Britain, France, Australia, New Zealand, Thailand, Pakistan, and the Philippines. It pledged to defend the countries of Southeast Asia against communist aggression. As a result of the wording of the treaty, and in contradiction to the Geneva accords, the southern half of Vietnam came to be recognized as a sovereign state, instead of as half of a temporarily divided nation, and was guaranteed SEATO assistance should it be invaded.

As a leader, Eisenhower almost always tried to steer a middle course between any two extremes. Vietnam was no exception. On the one hand, he refused to resort to the atomic bomb, or to commit American troops to the war. On the other, he refused to walk away and let all of Vietnam fall to the communists—an outcome that he believed would only encourage further communist aggression.

Not all of Eisenhower's problems were in the area of foreign policy. In May 1953 he found himself under intense pressure to stop the scheduled executions of convicted atomic spies Julius and Ethel Rosenberg. Individuals and groups of all political views from all over the world—including members of Eisenhower's own cabinet—tried to persuade him that the Rosenbergs were victims of the seething, often paranoid anticommunism of the time. Eisenhower listened carefully to the arguments favoring clemency for the couple. He said he was "impressed by all the honest doubt" of the Rosenbergs' guilt. He was absolutely unshaken, however, in his belief that they had exposed "literally millions of our citizens to death," and that their own deaths were necessary to deter others from spying for the Soviet Union. The Rosenbergs were electrocuted on June 19, 1953.

Meanwhile, Senator McCarthy, now head of a Senate investigating subcommittee, was pressing his quest for communists and communist sympathizers in the government. In his zeal, McCarthy even attacked the United States Army. He accused the army of promoting officers who were "Fifth-Amendment Communists." The Fifth Amendment to the U.S. Constitution guarantees each individual's right to refuse to testify against himself. According to McCarthy, a "Fifth-Amendment Communist" was anyone who refused to answer the questions of his subcommittee.

One confrontation in particular proved to be especially damaging to McCarthy's public image, and helped lead to his political downfall. During the televised hearing of June 9, 1954, McCarthy viciously attacked Patrick Fisher, an associate of army special counsel Joseph Welch. While a student at Harvard Law School, Fisher had joined the National Lawyers Guild, an organization subsequently named in connection with the Communist party. At the time of the hearing, Fisher was a respected associate of Welch's and secretary of the Young Republican League in Newton, Massachusetts. Before millions

Without exhaustive debate, even heated debate, of ideas and programs, free government would weaken and wither. But if we allow ourselves to be persuaded that every individual or party that takes issue with our own convictions is necessarily wicked or treasonous, then, indeed, we are approaching the end of freedom's road.
—DWIGHT D. EISENHOWER
in an address at Columbia
University, May 31, 1954

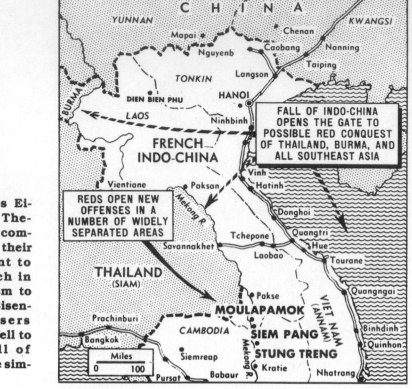

A 1954 map illustrates Eisenhower's "Domino Theory," which holds that communist nations export their system of government to other countries, which in turn spread communism to neighboring nations. Eisenhower and his advisers feared that if Vietnam fell to the communists, all of Southeast Asia would be similarly threatened.

of television viewers, Welch dramatically defended Fisher's reputation at the hearing, and in the process, shrewdly portrayed McCarthy as a cruel and reckless accuser bent on destroying the career of a promising young lawyer.

McCarthy had been a thorn in Eisenhower's side for a long time. He had attacked not only Eisenhower's old friend Marshall, but General Ralph Zwicker, a West Pointer who had been wounded during the D-Day invasion. McCarthy said that Zwicker was "not fit to wear" his uniform, and that he did not have "the brains of a five-year-old child." This outraged Eisenhower, but he still refused to condemn McCarthy in public. He thought to do so would give the senator additional importance and would cheapen the office of the presidency. It was not until McCarthy threatened to force members of the White House staff to testify before his subcommittee that Eisenhower finally took firm action.

The stand that Eisenhower took was one of "executive privilege." He believed the realities of the arms race and the Cold War required certain activities of government to remain secret. He said, therefore, that it would not be in the best interests of national security for members of the executive branch to testify about White House matters to any committee. No president had ever made such a claim. According to historian Arthur M. Schlesinger, jr., it was "the most absolute assertion of presidential right to withhold information from Congress ever uttered to that day . . . ."

Eisenhower's decision to invoke executive privilege, which denied McCarthy access to the witnesses he most wanted to cross-examine, reduced the army/McCarthy hearings to a series of increasingly wild and clearly unsubstantiated accusations. McCarthy's credibility and popularity dropped sharply, and in December 1954 he was censured by his colleagues for behavior unbecoming to the Senate. His long reign of fear and intimidation had finally come to an end.

Eisenhower talks with Vice-President Nixon in 1954. The president believed the arms race between the Soviet Union and the United States should be halted, and proposed an arms control program, called "Atoms for Peace." The Soviets remained skeptical, viewing the American disarmament proposal as part of America's interest in maintaining nuclear superiority.

With duffel bags slung on their backs, French troops board a transport at Tourane, or Da Nang. In July 1954 France formally surrendered at Geneva, Switzerland, after an eight-year struggle to retain its Vietnamese colony.

In spite of such conflicts and frustrations as the McCarthy situation, Eisenhower was enjoying his presidency. Since his boyhood years in Abilene, he had always wanted to be where the action was. He was used to working long, hard days, and he liked running the show. When he needed to relax, he would play golf or bridge with his small circle of close friends. He had also taken up oil painting. He no longer smoked cigarettes, never drank very much, and was endowed with great physical and mental energy.

Eisenhower was a proud grandfather. His son and daughter-in-law, John and Barbara, had had three children: Dwight David, Barbara Anne, and Susan Elaine. He and Mamie continued to be very close. At the White House, they slept in a custom-made double bed. Mamie once said she liked to reach over whenever she felt like it and "pat Ike on his old bald head."

Early in 1955, Eisenhower faced one of the biggest crises of his presidency. This one concerned the Nationalist Chinese, the Communist Chinese, and the two small islands of Quemoy and Matsu, which were located just off the coast of mainland China.

Following their defeat by the Chinese Communists in 1949, the Chinese Nationalists had abandoned the mainland and fled to the island of

Formosa. At the same time, they had occupied Quemoy and Matsu. Since then, they had been using the islands to stage raids against the mainland. Now, the Communist Chinese began shelling the islands. They were also threatening to invade Formosa itself. Tension over this issue mounted steadily through the early months of 1955.

In resolving this crisis, Eisenhower played a masterful game. He persuaded Congress to pass a resolution giving him the authority to defend Formosa with American troops whenever he decided it was necessary. This was the first time in history an American president had asked for and received advance permission from Congress to conduct a war as he saw fit. It gave Eisenhower a free hand, and it warned the Chinese Communists that America would intervene if they ever tried to invade Formosa.

Eisenhower had deliberately not mentioned Quemoy and Matsu in his resolution. Privately, he did not believe they were essential to the defense of Formosa. He also knew the only way he could turn back an invasion of the islands themselves was with tactical nuclear weapons—an option he was very reluctant to pursue. On the other hand, he did not want simply to relinquish Quemoy and Matsu to the Chinese Communists.

Eisenhower's resolution became known as his "Formosa Doctrine." When it was announced, observers were amazed that it contained no mention of Quemoy and Matsu. These two small islands were, after all, at the very heart of the crisis. Was Eisenhower going to defend them or not? Well, he would reply, maybe yes and maybe no. It would all depend on the circumstances. Whenever Eisenhower was asked to be more specific than that, he would deliberately be more vague.

By doing this, Eisenhower kept his options open and kept the Chinese Communists completely off balance. In the end, they decided not to invade Quemoy and Matsu—or Formosa. The threat of an atomic war gradually faded away. Eisenhower's bluff had worked. He had not been called "the best stud poker player in the army" for nothing.

In July 1955 Eisenhower and the leaders of the

> *If all Americans want is security they can go to prison. They'll have enough to eat, a bed, and a roof over their heads. But if an American wants to preserve his dignity and his equality as a human being, he must not bow his neck to any dictatorial government.*
> —DWIGHT D. EISENHOWER

Vietnamese communist leader Ho Chi Minh (1890–1969) organized Vietnam's successful war against French colonial forces. Eisenhower refused to recognize Ho's government in the northern part of Vietnam, and established the Southeast Asia Treaty Organization (SEATO) to defend the region from communism.

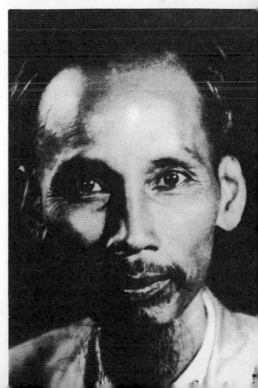

Soviet Union held a conference in Geneva. It was the first summit meeting since the end of World War II. Since then, relations between the two nations had gone from bad to worse. Each of the superpowers, determined to outdo the other, had continued to stockpile nuclear weapons at a terrifying rate. The world was, in Eisenhower's words, "racing toward catastrophe."

At the Geneva summit, Eisenhower made a second dramatic proposal to the Soviet leaders. He said he would give them a complete description of all the U.S. military facilities in exchange for a similar description of all Soviet military facilities. To assure accurate reports, each country would be allowed to conduct aerial photography over the other. Airfields would be provided for this purpose. Eisenhower's proposal was called "Open Skies." Much to his disappointment, the Soviets rejected it.

In the fall of 1955, Eisenhower suffered a heart attack. On vacation at a friend's ranch in Colorado, he had awakened in the middle of the night with terrible pains in his chest. Mamie quickly called a doctor, who had Eisenhower admitted to an army hospital in Denver.

Egyptian President Gamal Abdel Nasser (1918–1970) greets cheering crowds on July 28, 1954, after the British agreed to evacuate the Suez Canal zone. When Nasser nationalized the canal in 1956, the British and French asked the United States to help seize the canal; Eisenhower refused.

Map of the Suez Canal area. After Egypt closed the canal to Israeli shipping, Israel, Britain, and France invaded Egypt in an attempt to open the waterway. The Soviet Union, Egypt's ally, threatened to attack London and Paris with nuclear missiles. Eisenhower feared having to be an ally in a possible nuclear war.

Eisenhower stayed in the hospital for six weeks. He was a cheerful patient, determined to get well. He kept a close eye on the business of the country and shared the details of his condition with the American people. Mamie stayed in the hospital with him. As soon as Eisenhower was able to walk, he and Mamie returned to their farm in Gettysburg, Pennsylvania. (The Eisenhowers had purchased the farm in 1950. It was the first home they had ever owned.) There, Eisenhower continued to make a strong recovery.

With the 1956 election on the horizon, Eisenhower had to decide whether or not to run for a second term. He had suffered a serious heart attack and was now 65 years old. He liked the idea of retirement, but he also liked being president. His closest friends and advisers assured him he was the best man for the job. In February 1956, when his doctors told him he could expect to go on living an active life, Eisenhower announced that he would run.

Eisenhower was nominated at the Republican National Convention at San Francisco in August 1956. Again, Richard Nixon was nominated as his running mate. There were many celebrations, but Eisenhower had no time to enjoy them. The world was once more on the brink of war, this time in the Mideast.

Egypt's president, Gamal Abdel Nasser, had been negotiating for an international loan to help him build an immense dam at Aswan, on the Nile River. The United States had offered to lend more than $50 million. Nasser, however, was buying millions of dollars' worth of arms from Soviet-dominated countries, and was also trying to get better terms on a loan for the Aswan dam from the Soviet Union. Irritated by Nasser's dealings, the United States canceled its loan offer in July 1956.

Nasser retaliated by nationalizing the Suez Canal, which had been operated since 1888 by an inter-

The *Pollox* was one of the ships that Nasser sank as it entered the Suez Canal, in order to block the key passageway between the Mediterranean and Red Seas. The waterway was crucial since it linked trade routes among Europe, Asia, and the United States.

Eisenhower wears a traditional garland while bidding farewell to Chinese Nationalist President Chiang Kaishek (1887–1975). After the communists took over mainland China in 1949, the Nationalists fled to the islands of Formosa, Quemoy, and Matsu. Eisenhower threatened to intervene if the communists did not stop shelling these islands.

national company headed by the British. The Egyptian waterway, which links the Mediterranean with the Red Sea, was vital to international shipping. The British and the French, outraged by Nasser's taking over the canal, threatened to take it back by force, and urged the United States to help them.

Eisenhower had very special feelings for the British, who had been America's closest allies in World War II. Together, they had delivered the final blow to Hitler's armies on the Western Front. However, despite his natural affinity with the British, Eisenhower sincerely believed that the days of the colonial empires were over and that the British therefore had no legitimate claim to the Suez Canal. Nasser had promised to continue to operate the canal as an international waterway; with such a guarantee, Eisenhower saw no justification for the British to go to war with Egypt—and privately he told them so.

If Eisenhower was certain of one thing during the early days of the Suez crisis, it was that the British would never start a war in the Mideast without the support of the United States. As things turned out, he was mistaken.

Nasser had made clear his feelings toward Israel by supporting Arab guerrilla raids against the newly

I hate war as only a soldier who has lived it can, only as one who has seen its brutality, its futility, its stupidity.
—DWIGHT D. EISENHOWER

established Jewish nation. Three months after he nationalized the canal, he closed it to Israeli shipping. A few days later—on October 29, 1956—Israel, which had formed a secret alliance with Britain and France, invaded Egypt. A Franco-British assault on Egypt soon followed, prompting Nasser to block the canal by sinking dozens of ships that were in transit through it.

Meanwhile, the United States had introduced a cease-fire resolution for consideration by the United Nations. The resolution also called upon Israel to withdraw to its own borders. The American condemnation of Israel's actions astonished Britain and its allies, which had assumed that Eisenhower would side with them on the issue of the canal. The U.S. action also amazed—and delighted—the nations of the Third World, which had also expected Eisenhower to support America's traditional allies.

The Soviet response to the Israeli-British-French

A bust of Soviet leader Joseph Stalin, a cruel dictator who killed or imprisoned many of his own countrymen, is toppled and smashed in Budapest, Hungary. When, in 1956, Hungarian rebels rose up against Soviet domination, Eisenhower saw no wisdom in arming a revolt he believed could not succeed.

Hungarian citizens glumly watch Soviet tanks roll into their capital, Budapest. Hungarian freedom fighters stood little chance against massive Soviet military power. Many Americans were disappointed when Eisenhower did not airdrop weapons to the rebels, as recommended by the CIA.

assault on Egypt was one of anger. The Soviets, who were now major suppliers of money and war materials to Egypt, had become that country's most powerful ally. They threatened to join the war, and to launch nuclear missiles against London and Paris, unless the British and French withdrew from the Suez Canal.

Eisenhower was appalled. In spite of his work to defuse the crisis, the war was escalating. He issued a strong warning to the Soviets to stay out of the conflict or face American retaliation. However annoyed he might be with the British and French, Eisenhower could never side with the Soviets against them.

On election day, November 6, 1956, shortly after the Eisenhowers had cast their presidential votes at Gettysburg, the British and French agreed to a cease-fire. Eisenhower was immensely relieved. He had refused to support his friends in a cause he firmly believed was wrong. At the same time, he had kept the Soviet Union out of the battle. Threatened with a sharp cutback in American aid, Israel withdrew from Egypt. Nasser had agreed to reopen the canal. British and French troops soon left Egypt, and were replaced by a United Nations peacekeeping force. Once more, the world had pulled back from the brink of nuclear war.

During that nerve-wracking fall of 1956, Eisenhower had been so preoccupied with the international situation that he had hardly had time to remind himself that he was running for a second term. In the middle of the Suez crisis, there was also a crisis in Eastern Europe. Hungarian patriots, encouraged by radio broadcasts from the West, had staged a revolt against the Soviet domination of their country. The Soviets had responded by sending tanks into Budapest, the Hungarian capital. Popular opinion throughout the Western world enthusiastically supported the revolt. The CIA urged Eisenhower to airdrop weapons to the freedom fighters, who were hopelessly outnumbered and ill-equipped.

American soldiers returning from Germany read about Eisenhower's decision to run for a second term. After World War II ended, Germany was occupied by French, British, American, and Soviet forces. In 1955 the Allies granted self-government in the sectors of Germany they had controlled; the Soviets set up a communist government in East Germany.

I LIKE

IKE

A 1956 Eisenhower campaign button proclaims "I Like Ike." During a meeting to discuss Eisenhower's running for a second term, Eisenhower's secretary of state, John Foster Dulles (1889—1959), remarked that "there was no one person in the world who commanded the respect of as many people as did the president."

Eisenhower believed in the cause of the Hungarians, but he refused to go to their aid. His reasons were the practical reasons of a former general. Hungary was a landlocked country, surrounded by other Soviet satellite states, neutral Austria, and the Soviet Union itself. In any attempt by the United States to liberate Hungary—short of outright nuclear war—Eisenhower knew the Soviets would have an overwhelming advantage. The revolt was swiftly and brutally crushed. Many of the 200,000 Hungarians who became refugees settled in the United States— the country that had encouraged them to revolt, but that had been powerless to help them when they did.

In the 1956 presidential election, Eisenhower and Nixon ran against their previous Democratic opponent, Adlai Stevenson, and Stevenson's new running mate, Senator Estes Kefauver of Tennessee. When the votes were counted, Eisenhower and Nixon had won by an even bigger landslide than they had in 1952. And what the votes had declared was: "I like Ike!"

6

Crises Continue

As Eisenhower began his second term, the question of public-school desegregation dominated the news in the United States. It was an emotionally charged issue with deep and tragic roots in American history. Eisenhower was aware of these roots. In many ways, he had been shaped by them.

Following the Civil War, segregation laws had been enacted in the South to preserve "white supremacy." Known as "Jim Crow" laws, they forced black people to attend separate schools, use separate facilities in public places, and ride in separate sections in buses and railroad cars.

In 1896 the legality of "separate but equal" accommodations in railroad cars and train stations was upheld by the United States Supreme Court in the case of *Plessy* vs. *Ferguson*. This case became a model for other rulings in support of the Jim Crow laws. As a result, during the next 40 years, segregation became even more rigidly enforced throughout the South. It was also practiced in northern cities and towns—particularly in the areas of housing and education—and even in the nation's armed forces.

As the 1940s approached, opposition to the "separate but equal" doctrine increased throughout the

The crowd sings "We love Mamie" as President and Mrs. Eisenhower stand before supporters at New York City's Madison Square Garden, where Eisenhower delivered a major campaign address. Eisenhower and his wife had won not only votes, but the hearts of their audience as well.

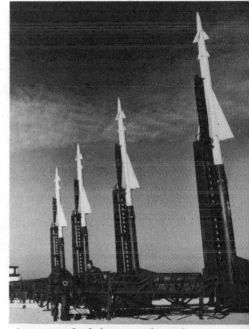

Army technicians make adjustments at a guided missile launching site near Washington, D.C. During Eisenhower's second term, many of his aides and constituents pressured him to increase arms research and production to keep pace with Soviet advances in rocket technology.

United States. Such opposition intensified during World War II, when many Americans began to become painfully aware of the obvious contradiction between supporting freedom and democracy overseas while maintaining segregation at home. This contradiction became even more obvious when black soldiers, confined to segregated units, fought bravely in defense of their country.

Throughout the 1940s, the civil rights movement continued to grow. In 1948 Truman ordered the gradual desegregation of the armed forces. By the time Eisenhower became president in 1953, civil rights advocates were working through the courts to desegregate the public schools. The issue was legally settled in May 1954 by the Supreme Court in the case of *Brown* vs. *the Board of Education of Topeka* (Kansas). Handing down its historic decision, the Court declared that the practice of racial segregation in public schools violated the Constitution of the United States.

The Supreme Court's ruling that public schools must be integrated created an explosive situation in the South. At the start of the school year in 1956, while Eisenhower was dealing with the Suez crisis and campaigning for a second term, the first attempts at desegregation began. There were incidents of mob violence in Tennessee and Texas. The governor of Texas openly defied the Court's orders. Other governors said they would do the same. The question quickly became: would the United States government use force, if necessary, to integrate the public schools? It was a question that Eisenhower very much hoped to avoid.

Throughout his political career, Eisenhower had been a consistent and outspoken supporter of black voting rights. He had never, however, been comfortable with the issue of integration. His own background probably accounts for this. Throughout most of his life, he had had few opportunities to associate with black people on anything like an equal basis. The Abilene of his boyhood years had been an all-white town. There had been no blacks at West Point when he was a cadet. From the day he was commissioned as a junior officer in 1915 to

There must be respect for the Constitution—which means the Supreme Court's interpretation of the Constitution—or we shall have chaos.

—DWIGHT D. EISENHOWER

the day he retired as a five-star general in 1948, he had served in a segregated army. He had lived for many years on bases in the South, and still went there to hunt and play golf. Powerful southern politicians had supported him as a candidate for the presidency. Some of his closest and most influential friends were southerners.

Nevertheless, in his first term, Eisenhower had completed the desegregation of the armed forces, begun by Truman. He had also desegregated all public facilities in Washington, D.C. He had not, however, agreed with the Supreme Court's decision in *Brown* vs. *the Board of Education*. He said he did not believe the human heart could be reformed by law. He thought any integration of public schools should be left up to the individual states, not to the federal government. In short, when it came to the crucial issue of desegregation, Eisenhower sympa-

Black sailors march in review before a white officer during World War II. In his first term as president, Eisenhower desegregated the armed forces. Although he supported equal opportunity "for every citizen" Eisenhower thought that the individual states—not the federal government—should decide whether to desegregate schools.

thized with the majority of southern whites who opposed it.

On September 3, 1957, a small number of black students, exercising their rights under the Constitution, tried to enter the previously all-white Central High School in Little Rock, Arkansas. The governor of Arkansas, Orval Faubus, had surrounded the school with troops from the state National Guard. The troops had orders to keep the black students from entering the school. The issue Eisenhower had hoped to avoid was now at hand.

Since the Supreme Court's decision in *Brown* vs. *the Board of Education*, public-school desegregation had become the law of the land. As president, Eisenhower knew he was sworn to uphold that law and, whatever his personal feelings might be, he fully intended to do so.

Reluctant to use force, Eisenhower first tried persuasion. In a private meeting on September 14, 1957, he warned Faubus that the state of Arkansas could not expect to win its fight with the federal government. Faubus seemed to agree, but did nothing to change the situation in Little Rock. There, tensions continued to mount for another week. Eisenhower, hoping the crisis would fade away, took no action. Finally, a federal judge ordered Faubus to stop trying to block integration at Central High School.

Unwilling to defy a direct federal order, Faubus withdrew his troops from the school. This took place on the weekend of September 21, 1957. Early the following Monday, hundreds of angry whites gathered in front of the school. When they learned that nine black students had entered the school through a side door, they became violent. They threatened to lynch the students and tried to cross police barricades. Unable to control the situation, Little Rock police removed the nine black students from the school. Still, Eisenhower took no action.

During the next 24 hours, the mobs in Little Rock grew from hundreds to thousands. The city's mayor sent Eisenhower an urgent telegram saying he had lost control of the city and needed federal troops to restore order. It was only at this late hour that Ei-

When National Guardsmen sent by Arkansas Governor Orval Faubus (b. 1919) and violent mobs barred nine black students from entering Central High School at Little Rock, Eisenhower ordered 1,000 paratroopers into the city to restore order.

senhower finally took action: he sent 1,000 paratroopers from the 101st Airborne Division into Little Rock. The paratroopers dispersed the mobs, and the nine black students safely reentered Central High School.

Essentially a matter of individual freedom and equality under the law, the issue of public-school desegregation would seem to have been tailor-made for a person like Eisenhower. His own integrity and decency were well known. As supreme commander he had led the fight against the tyranny of Hitler. In the Cold War with the Soviet Union, he had been a vigorous champion in the cause of freedom over slavery. But in the area of public-school desegregation, Eisenhower never provided the kind of forceful leadership the country desperately needed. Many historians have said this was his most significant flaw as president.

The tensions of Little Rock were only beginning to subside when the country found itself in a new turmoil—this time over the startling news that the Soviet Union had put the world's first man-made satellite into orbit. The name of the satellite, which had been carried into space by a rocket, was *Sputnik*. The Soviet feat convinced millions of Americans that the United States had fallen dangerously behind the Soviet Union in rocket technology. They believed this was not only a serious blow to American prestige but a major threat to the nation's security. Rockets that delivered satellites could also deliver bombs.

The nationwide uproar that followed *Sputnik*'s ascent bordered on panic. Eisenhower was deluged with demands that he sharply increase defense spending. The public wanted more accurate and longer-range missiles with more powerful nuclear warheads. Eisenhower was urged to begin a crash program to build fallout shelters that could protect American citizens in the event of a Soviet nuclear attack.

Eisenhower responded to the *Sputnik* crisis calmly. He said he thought the American people and many of his advisers were overreacting to the news of the Soviet satellite. He said he did not believe the

> *Golf symbolized the Eisenhower years—played by soft, boring men with ample waistlines who went around rich men's country-club courses in the company of wealthy businessmen and were tended by white-haired, dutiful Negroes.*
> —DAVID HALBERSTAM
> American journalist

A black student attempts to enter Little Rock Central High School but is blocked by National Guardsmen as whites opposed to desegregation shout insults at her. Eisenhower's leadership is thought to have been deficient regarding the segregation issue.

Soviet Union wanted to start a nuclear war. He dismissed the widespread complaints that there was a "missile gap," and expressed the opinion that fallout shelters would be of little use in the event of an all-out nuclear exchange. Eisenhower also refused to support radical increases in defense spending, saying the resulting deficits and inflation would do the country more harm than good. In Eisenhower's view, the goal was not to accelerate the arms race, but to halt it.

On November 25, 1957, while working at his desk in the Oval Office, Eisenhower suffered a stroke. He was 67 years old. When news of the stroke became public, many commentators urged him to resign; but he paid no attention to them. For two long, frustrating days, confined to his bedroom in the White House, he had trouble speaking. Then, through what seemed to Mamie and John a terrific effort of will, Eisenhower began to recover. The people who loved him were relieved and delighted. They told him that what he should do now was take a long vacation. Eisenhower paid no attention to this advice either, and very soon he was back at his desk.

The first national confrontation over desegregation was uneasily resolved when Eisenhower stationed soldiers at Little Rock's Central High School to ensure that black students were able to attend classes there. Stationed in or near the school were 500 paratroopers. Violent protesters were jailed.

Since the Suez crisis, President Nasser of Egypt had become an increasingly powerful force in the Mideast. He was a nationalist who believed strongly in Arab unity. Early in 1958, Nasser announced that Egypt had joined with Syria to form the United Arab Republic. Many of the Arab nations were still ruled by traditional monarchies. Nasser said he hoped these nations would overthrow their monarchies and join Egypt and Syria in the newly formed republic. This caused great tension in the Arab world. To counter Nasser, the kings of Jordan and Iraq formed a federation of their own.

The situation in the Mideast gave Eisenhower serious cause for concern. Nasser, though not a communist, had the support of the Soviet Union. So did Syria, with which Egypt was now united. Eisenhower knew that the more powerful Nasser became, the more influence the Soviet Union would have over the distribution of the Mideast's oil. This oil provided a primary and vital energy source to the Western world.

Eisenhower had already taken one step to make it clear that the United States was prepared to defend its interests in the Mideast. Early in his second term, he had persuaded Congress to give him authority to act swiftly in any Mideast crisis without waiting for congressional approval. This authority, intended to counter aggression in the area, became known as the "Eisenhower Doctrine."

In July 1958 pro-Nasser forces assassinated the royal family in Iraq. The kings of Jordan and Saudi Arabia feared that they might soon share similar fates themselves. To Western observers it seemed that Nasser's dream of uniting the Arab nations into a single federation was about to become a reality. Eisenhower believed the time had arrived to make a move in the Mideast. The place he picked to make the move was the small country of Lebanon.

Lebanon's domestic politics was largely determined by considerations of religion. Its two main faiths were Christianity and Islam. The country's president, Camille Chamoun, maintained friendly relations with the Western powers and was a Christian. He was under attack from Lebanese Muslims,

A smiling Eisenhower leaves after meeting with Arkansas Governor Orval Faubus (right). Eisenhower met with the governor to persuade him to let black students attend Little Rock Central High School in compliance with the Supreme Court's 1954 decision, *Brown* vs. *Board of Education of Topeka*, which made segregation in public schools illegal.

This Soviet cartoon depicts intense international interest in the world's first man-made satellite, *Sputnik*. The satellite surprised the West, and many Americans feared that *Sputnik* and the rocket used to launch the satellite might be used by the Soviets for military purposes.

Eisenhower was a subtle man, and no fool, though in pursuit of his objectives he did not like to be thought of as brilliant; people of brilliance, he thought, were distrusted.

—DAVID HALBERSTAM
American journalist

who felt, with some justification, that Chamoun had abused the power of his office. Fighting between Christian and Muslim militias had broken out in Beirut, the Lebanese capital. Chamoun had appealed to the United States for help. Eisenhower responded by ordering the Sixth Fleet, which was carrying a detachment of U.S. Marines, to take up positions off the coast of Lebanon. On July 15, 1958, he ordered the marines ashore.

When the marines landed in Lebanon, no shots were fired. Within a short time, elections were held and Chamoun was replaced by one of his Christian rivals. The political upheavals subsided. Neither the Egyptians nor the Soviet Union had tried to intervene on the side of the Lebanese Muslims. Eisenhower, satisfied that his show of force in the Mideast had been a success, withdrew the marines.

At home, political unrest continued to mount in the aftermath of *Sputnik*. The Democrats said the Republicans were responsible for the "missile gap," and for what they called the resulting loss of American security and prestige. The November 1958 midterm elections proved that the voters agreed with the Democrats. In spite of Eisenhower's personal popularity, which remained high, the Republicans suffered one of the worst defeats in their party's history.

Nikita Khrushchev, the new premier of the Soviet Union, quickly added to the growing anxiety of the American people. Less than a week after the 1958 election, he gave Eisenhower and the Western powers an ultimatum on Berlin—the former capital of Germany.

At the end of World War II, the Soviets had occupied the eastern sector of Berlin. The United States, with Britain and France, had occupied the western sector. The rights of the occupation forces had been established at the Yalta Conference. The city, located well inside the borders of Soviet dominated East Germany, had been a trouble spot ever since. In 1948 the Soviets had tested the will of the Allies to remain in Berlin by initiating a blockade of the city, cutting off all land and water routes into the western sector. The Allies had broken the blockade by flying over it. For 18 months, they had successfully supplied their half of the city by air. Finally, in 1949, the Soviets had lifted the blockade.

Now, 10 years later, Khrushchev suddenly announced that he was negotiating with the government of East Germany to end the occupation of Berlin. He said he expected the Allies to do the same. He said he wanted Berlin to become a "free city" within six months, and called for all foreign troops to withdraw. The United States was strongly committed to the people of West Berlin. To many Americans, it looked as though the final confrontation of the Cold War was about to begin. A sense of alarm swept the country. The pressures on Eisenhower to increase defense spending and take drastic measures against the Soviet Union continued to mount.

Eisenhower refused to yield to these pressures. His response to the crisis was balanced but firm. Unlike many of his top advisers, he did not believe the Soviet Union was ready to go to war over West Berlin. Through the early months of 1959, as Khrushchev's deadline approached, Eisenhower made it

Troops guard the royal palace after the assassination in 1958 of Iraq's royal family by supporters of Egypt's President Nasser and the United Arab Republic he formed with Syria earlier that year. Western governments worried that Arab unification directed by Nasser and his Soviet allies would affect oil exports.

increasingly clear to the Soviet leader that the Allies had no intention of pulling out of the city. At the same time, he said he was willing to discuss the problem in a reasonable way. He also said he might agree to a summit meeting with Khrushchev—something he had previously been reluctant to do.

As a result of Eisenhower's balanced approach, the crisis in Berlin faded away. Khrushchev withdrew his deadline. There was no war. The western sector of the city remained free.

When Eisenhower looked out at the world during his second term, what he saw was change. The French had lost their war in Vietnam. The British had failed to keep control of the Suez Canal. The old colonial empires were continuing to break apart. Throughout the Third World, new nations were being born as colonies achieved independence.

The Soviet Union and Communist China were working to increase their influence in the Third World. Eisenhower believed it was essential for the United States to do the same. He thought the best method was through economic aid. The majority of Americans disagreed. So did a majority in Congress. To them, investing money in weapons made sense, investing in the futures of developing countries did not. As hard as he tried, Eisenhower was never able to convince the nation that its own interests would be best served by a generous program of foreign aid.

Following the 1958 Berlin crisis, relations between the United States and the Soviet Union began to improve. The two superpowers seemed to be moving toward an agreement to ban nuclear testing in the atmosphere and to begin serious discussions on disarmament.

In September 1959, responding to an invitation from Eisenhower, Khrushchev visited the United States. The Soviet premier was a colorful figure, sometimes friendly, sometimes belligerent, who spoke loudly of his desire for peace. He and Eisenhower agreed to hold a summit meeting in the near future. Khrushchev invited Eisenhower to visit the Soviet Union with his family. Eisenhower accepted the invitation, saying he would arrange to take the trip shortly after the summit.

President Eisenhower and Soviet Premier Nikita Khrushchev (1894–1971) stand at attention as a band plays the American and Soviet national anthems during Khrushchev's 1959 visit to the U.S. The visit went well, and expectations were high that disarmament talks and a lasting peace were within reach.

Eisenhower's greatest hope as he began the final year of his presidency was for a secure peace and an end to the Cold War. In February 1960, against the counsel of his military advisers, he offered to sign a nuclear test-ban treaty with the Soviet Union. The Soviet response to this significant proposal was positive. The long-awaited summit meeting between Eisenhower and Khrushchev was scheduled to be held in Paris in the middle of May. As the summit approached, Eisenhower's hopes for a lasting peace had never been so high.

Then, on May 1, 1960, in the eighth year of his presidency, Eisenhower suffered what was, perhaps, the heaviest blow of his career.

Four years earlier, Eisenhower had authorized the CIA to fly secret high-altitude reconnaissance missions over the Soviet Union. These flights were carried out in a specially designed type of aircraft called the U-2. The planes, equipped with high-resolution telescopic cameras, were based in West Germany and several other NATO countries. The Soviets had tracked the U-2 flights with radar and had protested against them many times. The United States, aware of the fact that the Soviets had no interceptor aircraft or antiaircraft missiles capable

Government soldiers battle Muslim insurgents in the city of Tripoli. On Eisenhower's order U.S. Marines landed in Lebanon after Muslim militiamen rebelled against their Christian president, Camille Chamoun. Eisenhower demonstrated to Egypt's President Nasser and to the Soviets that, if pressured, he would use force in the region.

of reaching the U-2's operating altitude (65,000 feet) and that they could, therefore, neither engage nor identify the intruders, had always denied that the flights were taking place.

From the start, Eisenhower had had mixed feelings about the U-2 operation. On the one hand, he knew it was a seriously provocative act to violate the airspace of another country. On the other hand, the information he was getting from the U-2 flights—particularly regarding the number and location of Soviet missile sites—was important to the security of the United States.

In the spring of 1960, two weeks before the Paris summit was to begin, Eisenhower temporarily suspended the U-2 program. The last flight he authorized took off from a base in Turkey on the morning of May 1. That afternoon, Eisenhower received word that the plane was missing somewhere over the Soviet Union. Four days later, Khrushchev announced in an angry speech that the Soviet Union had shot down a "bandit" spy plane from the United States. Khrushchev said it should now be obvious to the world that the Americans, by their provocative actions, were trying to sabotage the Paris summit before it began.

Eisenhower denied Khrushchev's charges. Because the Soviet premier had once again presented no proof that the spy flight had actually taken place, Eisenhower assumed he had no proof. The unmarked plane, equipped with special explosive devices, must have been destroyed, and the pilot, who carried no identification, must have been killed. Based on these assumptions, Eisenhower approved an official statement saying that a U.S. "weather reconnaissance" plane had experienced trouble over Turkey and may have accidentally strayed into Soviet airspace. This innocent weather plane, the statement said, must have been the one the Soviets were talking about.

Khrushchev responded the next day by showing what he claimed was a photograph of the wrecked U-2. Expert analysts from the CIA quickly pointed out that the wreckage was not of a U-2 at all, but of a completely different type of plane. Eisenhower had gambled by denying the spy flight had ever taken place. Now he was sure his gamble had worked, and that Khrushchev was bluffing. The false photograph seemed to prove it. So Eisenhower repeated what he had said in the first place: the United States was not sending high-altitude spy planes over the Soviet Union.

Eisenhower had been a gambler all his life, and many of his gambles had paid off. But this time, he had badly misjudged his opponent. Khrushchev's photograph of the false wreckage had been a trap. He had reasoned that, if confident that no proof of the plane's mission existed, the United States would strike an indignant pose, claim to be falsely accused, and maybe even go so far as to demand an apology.

The Soviet premier waited for two days while the United States, now sure that no proof would be forthcoming, continued to deny that it was conducting spy flights over the Soviet Union. Then Khrushchev triumphantly announced that he not only had the actual wreckage of the U-2 to prove his claim, but that he also had the plane's pilot, Francis Gary Powers, who, in Khrushchev's own words, was "alive and kicking"—and now a prisoner—in Moscow. The Soviet Union had developed a missile capable of bringing down U-2s.

During the next 48 hours, Eisenhower and his administration issued evasive and confusing statements regarding the U-2 flight. Finally, in a meeting with the leaders of Congress, Eisenhower admitted that his cover-up had failed to work. He revealed the history of the U-2 flights, saying they had provided him with essential intelligence. In a lame attempt to justify his administration's breach of faith, he pointed out that, ever since *Sputnik*, the Soviets had had reconnaissance satellites that regularly orbited over the United States. In spite of Eisenhower's belated explanations, however, the damage had been done.

At the Paris summit, which was held the following week, an irate Khrushchev said he no longer wanted Eisenhower to visit the Soviet Union. The summit ended when Khrushchev and the Soviet delegation abruptly walked out. Eisenhower's dream of secur-

Francis Gary Powers, the pilot of a U-2 high-altitude spy plane, was shot down while flying an espionage mission over the Soviet Union. After Eisenhower denied that such flights were made over the Soviet Union, Khrushchev revealed that the plane's American pilot had been captured alive.

Soviet Premier Nikita Khrushchev denounced the United States after storming out of the Paris summit in May 1960. The U-2 spy plane incident shattered the possibilities for improved relations between the two superpowers. Eisenhower's attempts to cover up the spy flight caused Khrushchev to cancel future talks.

This conjunction of an immense military establishment and a large arms industry is new in the American experience. . . . We recognize the imperative need for this development. Yet we must not fail to comprehend its grave implications. In the councils of government, we must guard against the acquisition of unwarranted influence, whether sought or unsought, by the military-industrial complex. The potential for the disastrous rise of misplaced power exists and will persist.
—DWIGHT D. EISENHOWER
in his farewell address to
the American people,
January 17, 1961

ing a lasting peace had been shattered by the incident, and by his own ill-advised and unsuccessful attempt to cover it up.

Through the remaining months of Eisenhower's second term, relations between the United States and the Soviet Union were as bad as they had ever been. The Cold War was once again in full swing. Khrushchev formed alliances with Patrice Lumumba, prime minister of the Congo (the newly independent African nation, known since 1971 as Zaire), and with Premier Fidel Castro in Cuba. Eisenhower responded by authorizing covert CIA operations aimed at overthrowing Castro and Lumumba and replacing them with leaders friendly to the West. In the autumn of 1960, Khrushchev denounced the United States at the United Nations; he was so angry that at one point he took off his shoe and pounded it on the table.

The Twenty-Second Amendment to the Constitution, ratified in 1951, limits a president to two terms. Eisenhower knew his days in the White House were drawing to a close. He was still popular with millions of Americans, but there was a sense throughout the country that people were ready for a change.

The Democrats had nominated John F. Kennedy, a young senator from Massachusetts, to lead their ticket against the Republican nominee, Vice-President Richard Nixon. Kennedy had commanded a P-T boat in the Pacific during World War II. When the boat was rammed by a Japanese destroyer, Kennedy had helped save the life of one of the crew. Later, he had written a book entitled *Profiles in Courage*, which had won a Pulitzer Prize. Attractive and articulate, Kennedy spoke of the need to get the country moving again. Late in the campaign, he debated Nixon on national television. This was the first debate of its kind. Though Nixon did well on the issues, he was no match for the dynamic and appealing Kennedy. The November 8, 1960, election was extremely close, but the voters chose John F. Kennedy to be the 35th president of the United States.

Before leaving office in January 1961, Eisenhower delivered a farewell address to the American people. In his speech, which was carried live on national radio and television, Eisenhower spoke of the powerful military establishment that had developed in the country since World War II, and of the enormous armaments industry that had grown up to serve it. He said the influence of this "military-industrial complex" was now being felt "in every city, every statehouse, every office of federal government." He warned the American people that, with billions of dollars at stake, this kind of influence could easily be abused, and he urged them to be ever watchful in protecting their freedoms and liberties.

Three days later, on an inauguration day that was bitter cold in the nation's capital, Eisenhower stepped down from the presidency and John F. Kennedy took over.

After a lifetime of service to his country, Dwight D. Eisenhower was once again a private citizen. Under his leadership the nation had weathered many crises, and had known eight years of prosperity and peace. This is what Eisenhower had promised when he had first run for office in 1952. In spite of his disappointments, he had done his job well. Now he looked forward to enjoying his retirement years with Mamie.

As the Eisenhowers drove away from Washington on that cold day in January 1961, neither of them could have imagined that the world Eisenhower had done so much to shape was about to come apart.

Fidel Castro (b. 1926) seized control of Cuba in 1959 after waging a two-year guerrilla war against the corrupt government of Fulgencio Batista (1901–1973). When Castro sought an alliance with the Soviet Union, Eisenhower asked the CIA to begin planning to overthrow the Cuban leader.

7

An Old Soldier in a New Age

The decade of the 1960s was one of the most tumultuous in U.S. history. Some of the seeds Eisenhower had planted grew to bear bitter and unexpected fruit. John F. Kennedy had scarcely taken office before the country experienced a crisis over Cuba. There, a paramilitary force made up of Cuban exiles, initially sponsored by the CIA, tried to invade the island in hopes of overthrowing the revolutionary, left-wing government of Fidel Castro. Denied close air support by Kennedy, who wanted to conceal U.S. involvement, the invaders were easily overwhelmed by Castro's forces at the Bay of Pigs.

The Soviet Union, encouraged by Castro and by the botched invasion attempt, began to install nuclear missiles in Cuba. Kennedy responded by surrounding the island with a naval blockade, warning the Soviets that the missiles (which were not yet operational) must be withdrawn. The Soviets finally yielded, but not before the world had moved closer than it ever had to the brink of nuclear war.

At home, the issue of civil rights continued to boil. In October 1962 white mobs rioted when James Meredith became the first black student to enter the

President Eisenhower strolls on his 550-acre farm in Gettysburg, Pennsylvania, where he and his wife retired after he left the Oval Office in January 1961. Eisenhower disagreed with many decisions made by his Democratic successors, John F. Kennedy (1917–1963) and Lyndon Baines Johnson (1908–1973).

Eisenhower was pleased when his former vice-president, Richard Nixon, defeated the Democratic nominee, Hubert H. Humphrey (1911–1978), in the 1968 presidential election. Eisenhower remarked in 1967, "I cannot think of anyone better prepared than Dick Nixon is to undertake the responsibilities of the presidency."

University of Mississippi. It took 3,000 troops to restore order. In August 1963 nearly a quarter of a million Americans gathered in Washington to support black demands for equal rights. In June 1964 three civil rights workers were murdered in the South. Race riots eventually broke out in Los Angeles, Newark, and Detroit. More than 100 people died in these riots, thousands were injured, and millions of dollars' worth of property was destroyed.

In Vietnam, the North Vietnamese communists, denied the elections promised by the Geneva accords, set out to take South Vietnam by force. As a result, Kennedy increased to 16,000 the number of American troops in this small Southeast Asian country that Eisenhower had helped create. Year after year, under three presidents, the war in Vietnam would continue to escalate. The number of U.S. troops would eventually reach close to half a million. By the late 1960s thousands of Americans protested the war by demonstrating on college campuses and in the streets of the nation's capital. The Vietnam war divided the country more bitterly than any issue since slavery and the Civil War.

The chaos of the 1960s cut to the very heart of political life in America. On November 22, 1963, less than three years after he had succeeded Eisenhower as president, John F. Kennedy was assassinated while riding in a motorcade in Dallas, Texas. His successor, Lyndon Baines Johnson, was elected to a full term as president in 1964, but he declined to run for a second term due to the bitter controversy over Vietnam. On April 4, 1968, civil rights leader Martin Luther King, Jr., was assassinated on a motel balcony in Memphis, Tennessee. Two months later, John F. Kennedy's younger brother Robert was shot dead in Los Angeles while campaigning for the presidency.

As Eisenhower watched the 1960s unfold, it seemed to him the country had lost all its moorings and was drifting without a rudder on a stormy and dangerous sea. He was appalled that Kennedy had not provided close air support for the invasion force at Cuba's Bay of Pigs. He could not understand why Johnson followed a policy of gradual escalation in

What he would have liked said of him is that he achieved the highest objective of his or any other modern presidency: in a nuclear world, teeming with violence on all sides, he successfully 'waged peace' for the eight years of his incumbency.
—ARTHUR LARSON
American historian

the Vietnam war. These were military matters, and Eisenhower was first and foremost a military man.

As president, Eisenhower had committed the United States to the defense of South Vietnam. To him, the people who demonstrated against the war were acting in a way that bordered on treason. He had no patience with the long-haired "hippies" who seemed to him to have lost any semblance of morality, and who openly experimented with drugs. He deplored the decline of traditional manners, and of respect for law and order.

Eisenhower was retired now; though he remained

U.S Airborne Division troops leap from a helicopter into territory held by Vietnamese communist forces. American public opinion was split over the war in Vietnam. World War II and the Korean War veterans—including Eisenhower—were appalled when young men resisted the draft and protested America's involvement in the conflict.

keenly interested in the affairs of the world, he no longer carried the burdens of leadership. When he and Mamie had left the White House, they had taken up residence at their 550-acre Gettysburg farm. For the first time in their marriage they were able to be with each other constantly. Their bond was affectionate and strong. They would spend hours there in the glassed-in sunporch at the farm, reading, watching television, enjoying the beauty of the countryside.

John and Barbara Eisenhower, who now had four children, lived on the Gettsyburg property, less than a mile from the senior Eisenhowers. There were pet dogs on the farm, riding horses, prize Angus cattle, crops of soybeans, sorghum, oats, and hay. The children loved being on the farm. Eisenhower loved having them there.

Eisenhower wrote several books during his retirement, including the memoirs of his presidency. His son John, who had worked closely with him for many years, helped with the research. In addition to his memoirs, Eisenhower wrote an autobiography entitled, *At Ease: Stories I Tell to Friends*. One of the stories was of the time when, as a boy, he had gone to visit his Aunt Minnie and Uncle Luther's farm in Topeka, and had had to chase away a hostile gander with his broom.

In April 1968 Eisenhower suffered a major heart attack. His health had been gradually failing for a long time. He was taken to Walter Reed Army Hospital in Washington, D.C., where he would spend the final year of his life. Mamie stayed in a small room next to his. Aware that many women had begun to question the traditional roles in marriage, she never questioned her own. "I was Ike's wife, John's mother, the children's grandmother," she once said. "That's all I ever wanted to be."

In his hospital room, Eisenhower received many visitors and continued to keep a sharp eye on the world. In 1968 his former vice-president, Richard Nixon, had won the Republican nomination and was running against Lyndon Johnson's vice-president, Hubert Humphrey. Eisenhower was delighted when Nixon won in November. (He was also pleased

There is, in our affairs at home, a middle way between untrammeled freedom of the individual and the demands for the welfare of the whole nation.
—DWIGHT D. EISENHOWER

Dr. Henry Kissinger (b. 1923), President Nixon's adviser on national security affairs, confers with the president in the White House. Kissinger subsequently became secretary of state, and negotiated with North Vietnamese leaders during the Vietnam War.

that, during the campaign, his grandson, David Eisenhower, was spending more and more time with Nixon's daughter Julie.)

David and Julie were married in December. Eisenhower, now 78 years old, watched the ceremony on closed-circuit television from his hospital room. Over 50 years had passed since he had married Mamie Doud at her parents' elegant home in Denver, and had cut the wedding cake with his sword.

Eisenhower died in his room at Walter Reed Army Hospital on the morning of March 28, 1969. He was buried in Abilene, Kansas, not far from his childhood home.

A recent poll of American historians rated Dwight D. Eisenhower one of the 10 greatest presidents in the history of the United States.

Eisenhower undoubtedly left his mark on his country and on the world.

U.S. Air Force B-52s bomb communist targets during the Vietnam War. The war that Eisenhower believed would imperil all Southeast Asia finally ended in 1975 when the North Vietnamese army routed South Vietnamese troops and occupied Saigon. America had lost a costly war that had deeply divided the nation.

The funeral of President Dwight David Eisenhower. Eisenhower died of natural causes on March 28, 1969. After serving his country for 20 years as a military leader and president, Eisenhower's last words were, "I want to go; God take me."

Further Reading

Ambrose, Stephen E. *Eisenhower, Volume One: Soldier, General of the Army, President-Elect, 1890–1952.* New York: Simon and Schuster, 1983.

——. *Eisenhower, Volume Two: The President.* New York: Simon and Schuster, 1984.

Brandon, Dorothy. *Mamie Doud Eisenhower.* New York: Charles Scribner's Sons, 1954.

Davis, Kenneth S. *Soldier of Democracy: A Biography of Dwight Eisenhower.* Garden City, New York: Doubleday, Doran & Co., 1945.

Eisenhower, Dwight D. *At Ease: Stories I Tell to Friends.* Garden City, New York: Doubleday & Co., Inc., 1967.

——. *Crusade in Europe.* Garden City, New York: Doubleday & Co., Inc., 1948.

——. *Letters to Mamie,* ed. John S. D. Eisenhower. Garden City, New York: Doubleday & Co., Inc., 1978.

McCann, Kevin. *Man from Abilene.* Garden City, New York: Doubleday & Co., Inc., 1952.

Neal, Steve. *The Eisenhowers: Reluctant Dynasty.* Garden City, New York: Doubleday & Co., Inc., 1978.

Summersby, Kay. *Eisenhower Was My Boss.* Englewood Cliffs, New Jersey: Prentice-Hall, Inc., 1948.

Chronology

Oct. 14, 1890	Born Dwight David Eisenhower in Denison, Texas
June 1915	Graduates from the United States Military Academy at West Point
July 1, 1916	Marries Mamie Doud in Denver, Colorado
1920–40	Serves as staff officer in U.S. Army
1941–42	Oversees, as a brigadier general, domestic planning for American war effort in the Far East
June 11, 1942	Appointed commander of European theater of operations
1942–43	Directs "Operation Torch," the Allied campaign against German forces in North Africa
June 6, 1944	D-Day: Gives order to launch—and commands—the Allied invasion of Normandy
May 7, 1945	Accepts surrender of German armies
Feb. 7, 1948	Retires from the army, a five-star general
1948–50	Serves as president of Columbia University
Oct. 1950	Appointed to command the forces of the North Atlantic Treaty Organization (NATO)
Jan. 20, 1953	Inaugurated as 34th president of the United States after winning election against Adlai Stevenson II
July 1953	North Korean communists and United Nations forces sign truce at Panmunjom, ending the Korean War
Dec. 8, 1953	Eisenhower proposes Soviet-American discussion of nuclear disarmament in "Atoms for Peace" speech at the U.N.
July 1955	Submits "Open Skies" proposal to the Geneva summit
Nov. 1956	Helps to defuse Suez crisis Refuses to intervene as Soviet tanks crush Hungarian revolt
Nov. 6, 1956	Elected to second term as president of the United States
Sept. 24, 1957	Orders federal troops into Little Rock, Arkansas, to guarantee safety of nine black students enrolling at a previously all-white high school
July 15, 1958	Sends U.S. Marines ashore in Lebanon to quell Muslim-Christian hostilities
May 1960	Soviet Premier Nikita Khrushchev walks out of Paris summit following U-2 incident
Jan. 17, 1961	Eisenhower delivers farewell address in which he warns against the "military-industrial complex"
March 28, 1969	Dies, aged 78, of natural causes, at Walter Reed Army Hospital in Washington, D.C.

Index

Abilene, Kansas, 21, 24, 25, 27, 33, 61, 78, 90

Allied Expeditionary Force, 13, 15, 16, 19, 45–49, 51, 55–56

Allies see Allied Expeditionary Force

Ambrose, Stephen E., 70

"Atlantic Wall," 15

"Atoms for Peace" proposal, 70

Battle of the Bulge, 56–57

Bay of Pigs, 105, 106

Belgium, 13, 55, 62

Berlin, 56, 97–98

Brown vs. the Board of Education of Topeka, 90

Calais, 51

Casablanca, 47

Castro, Fidel, 102, 105

Central Intelligence Agency (CIA), 72, 82, 99, 100, 102, 105

Chamoun, Camille, 95–96

Churchill, Winston, 8, 45, 55

"Citizens for Eisenhower," 63

civil rights movement, 89–93, 106

Civil War, 89, 106

Clark Field, 41

Cold War, 71, 93, 96, 97, 99, 102

Columbia University, 62, 65

communism, 64, 65

concentration camps, 57

Congo, 102

Conner, Fox, 35

Constasino, Mario, 8

Crusade in Europe, 62

Cuba, 73, 102, 105
    see also Bay of Pigs

Dallas, Texas, 104

Darlan, Jean, 48

Davis, Bob, 25

D-Day, 17, 76

de Gaulle, Charles, 98

de Tocqueville, Alexis, 9, 11

Democracy in America, 9

Democratic party, 61, 63, 65, 97, 102

Denison, Texas, 19, 21

Denver, Colorado, 32–33, 78

desegregation, 89

Detroit, Michigan, 106

Doud, Mary Geneva, 32
    see also Eisenhower, Mamie

Dulles, John Foster, 69

Egypt, 85, 95

Eisenhower, Dwight
    birth, 20
    civil rights and, 89–93
    commander of European theater of operations, 44–58
    commander of the North Atlantic Treaty Organization (NATO), 62
    death, 110
    early years, 21–27
    education, 29–31
    Korean War and, 68–69
    literary career, 62, 108
    McCarthyism and, 75–77
    president, 61–87, 89–103
    president of Columbia University, 62
    presidential campaigns, 65–67, 85
    retirement from army, 62

Eisenhower, Arthur (Dwight Eisenhower's brother), 21, 24

Eisenhower, David (Dwight Eisenhower's father), 19, 20, 21, 23, 27, 43

Eisenhower, David Dwight (Dwight Eisenhower's son), 33

Eisenhower, Earl (Dwight Eisenhower's brother), 62

Eisenhower, Edgar (Dwight Eisenhower's brother), 62

Eisenhower, Ida (Dwight Eisenhower's mother), 19–25, 27, 62

Eisenhower, John Sheldon Doud (Dwight Eisenhower's son), 33, 38, 54

Eisenhower, Mamie (Dwight Eisenhower's wife), 33, 38, 54, 58, 61, 67, 80, 94, 103
    see also Doud, Mary Geneva

Eisenhower, Roy (Dwight Eisenhower's brother), 60

"Eisenhower Doctrine," 95

Emerson, Ralph Waldo, 10, 11

English Channel, 15–16, 74

"falling domino" theory, 74

Faubus, Orval, 92

Federalist Papers, 10

Fisher, Patrick,   75
Formosa,   79
"Formosa Doctrine,"   79
Fort Sam Houston,   32, 33, 39
France,   13, 33, 36, 45, 47, 48, 50, 51, 55,
     62, 97
Geneva,   74, 80
Germany,   20, 33, 36, 39, 45, 47, 58, 97, 99
Gettysburg, Pennsylvania,   81
Great Britain,   13, 36, 45, 54, 62, 72, 83, 85,
     97
Hazlett, Everett,   26
Hiroshima,   59, 70
Hitler, Adolf,   8, 15, 49, 56, 93
Ho Chi Minh,   73, 74
Humphrey, Hubert H.,   108
Hungary,   86–87
Iran,   72
Israel,   84
Italy,   39, 49
James, William,   8
Japan,   36, 42, 59
Jews,   49, 57
Jim Crow laws,   89
Jodl, Alfred,   58
Johnson, Lyndon Baines,   106, 108
Kefauver, Estes,   87
Kennedy, John F.,   102, 103, 105, 106, 108
Kennedy, Robert,   106
Khrushchev, Nikita,   97–98, 100–102
King, Martin Luther, Jr.,   106
Korean War,   68–69
Krueger, Walter,   38
Laos,   73
Lebanon,   95–96
Lecompton, Kansas,   20
Lenin, Vladimir,   8
Letters to Mamie,   59
Lincoln, Abraham,   11
Little Rock, Arkansas,   92–93
London,   45, 50, 56, 85
Lumumba, Patrice,   102
MacArthur, Douglas,   35–36, 41, 43, 69
Marshall, George C.,   35, 41, 42, 44, 45, 49
Marxism,   7, 8
Matsu,   79
McCarthy, Joseph,   65, 66, 75–76, 77

Mennonites,   20
Meredith, James,   105
Merrifield, Wesley,   24
Montgomery, Bernard,   55
Moscow,   101
Mossadegh, Mohammed,   72
Nagasaki,   57
Nasser, Gamal Abdel,   82, 95
New York Times,   30
Niebuhr, Reinhold,   10
Nixon, Richard,   66, 68, 82, 103
Normandy,   13, 52
North Atlantic Treaty Organization (NATO),
     62, 74, 99
North Korea,   64, 69
North Vietnam,   106
"Open Skies" proposal,   80
"Overlord" operation,   50
Pahlavi, Mohammed Reza,   72
Panmunjom,   69
Paris,   34, 99–101
Past Forgetting: My Love Affair with Dwight
     D. Eisenhower,   59
Patton, George,   52, 55
Pearl Harbor,   39, 41, 43
People's Republic of China,   78–79
Pershing, John,   35–36
Philippines,   34, 36, 38, 41, 43
Poland,   36
Portsmouth,   52
Powers, Francis Gary,   101
Profiles in Courage,   103
Quemoy,   79
Republican party,   61, 70, 97
Rommel, Erwin,   15, 50
Roosevelt, Franklin D.,   43, 50, 54, 57, 65
Rosenberg, Ethel,   75
Rosenberg, Julius,   75
San Antonio, Texas,   32, 33
Schlesinger, Arthur M., jr.,   77
Sicily,   49
South Korea,   64, 69
South Vietnam,   106, 107
Southeast Asia Treaty Organization (SEATO),
     74
Sputnik,   93, 96, 101
Stalin, Joseph,   46

Stevenson, Adlai E., II, 65–66, 87
Suez Canal, 82, 98
Suez Crisis, 82–85, 90, 95
Summersby, Kay, 58–59
Syria, 95
Taft, Robert, 63
Thorpe, Jim, 30
Tolstoy, Leo, 7
Topeka, Kansas, 21, 27, 90
"Torch" operation, 45, 46
Truman, Harry S., 59, 61, 65, 90, 91, 99
U-2 incident, 99–101
Union of Soviet Socialist Republics (U.S.S.R.),
      33, 45, 54, 62, 63, 70–71, 72, 80–83,
      86, 93, 95–101, 105
United Arab Republic, 95
United Nations, 64, 70, 102
United States Army, 19, 30, 37, 52
United States Marines, 96
United States Military Academy at West Point,
      27, 29–31, 91

United States Naval Academy, 27
United States Supreme Court, 65, 90
Vichy, 48
Vietnam, 73, 98, 106
Vietnam War, 106, 107
Wainwright, Jonathan M., 43
War and Peace, 7
Washington, D.C., 38, 91
Welch, Joseph, 75
Wilson, Woodrow, 8
World War I, 33, 43
World War II
      Eastern Front, 45
      European theater, 13–17, 44–45,
            50–51, 54–58
      North African campaigns, 45–50
      Pacific Front, 41–43, 59
Yalta Conference, 65, 97
Zangara, Guiseppe, 8
Zhukov, Georgi, 64
Zwicker, Ralph, 76

Peter Lars Sandberg is a novelist and short story writer. His work has appeared in *Best American Short Stories, Playboy, McCall's, Saturday Review, The Literary Review,* and *Scholastic Magazine.* He and his wife Nancy spend their winters in Virginia and their summers in New Hampshire.

Arthur M. Schlesinger, jr., taught history at Harvard for many years and is currently Albert Schweitzer Professor of the Humanities at City University of New York. He is the author of numerous highly praised works in American history and has twice been awarded the Pulitzer Prize. He served in the White House as special assistant to Presidents Kennedy and Johnson.